G000126406

A IS FOR ARSON

A Suffragette Alphabet
of Rebellion & Resistance

Written by Jack Joslin
Illustrated by Cat Crossley

CLAVIS &
CLAUSTRA

THE TIME IS NOW

Enough is enough. Women still do not have the vote despite decades of peaceful petitioning. Even so-called "progressive" political allies offer nothing but tepid support.

Call it frustration or call it fury – something is stirring beneath the rigid class system and respectable veneer of Edwardian Britain. More and more are drawn to the clear and simple demand: Votes for Women.

Emmeline Pankhurst establishes the WSPU (Women's Social and Political Union) in 1903. This is when things start heating up. Righteous anger builds and builds. What begins as a flicker becomes a wildfire.

From 1905, campaigners for women's suffrage take action. Polite protest is not working. It's time to stop asking and start fighting. Deeds, not words.

The press come up with a belittling term for these "hysterical" and "violent cranks": suffragettes. It's short and snappy. The WSPU steal it, turning the name into a badge of honour.

The suffragettes strike deep into the heart of an unjust society with increasingly dangerous and daring acts of resistance. From A to Z, witness the revolution that changed the course of history forever.

"I incite this meeting to rebellion."
– Emmeline Pankhurst

A IS FOR ARSON

"It is not only war we have declared," says Christabel Pankhurst. "We are fighting for a revolution!"

Facing a government which cares more about property than it does for women's lives, the suffragettes write their rebellion in fire.

Popular venues including disused churches, cricket pavilions, and railway stations are set alight while empty, forcing an apathetic public to take notice.

A campaign of arson – not always sanctioned by the leadership – reduces establishment emblems to embers. The message is clear: the suffragettes will not quietly fade away.

A single spark can start an inferno.

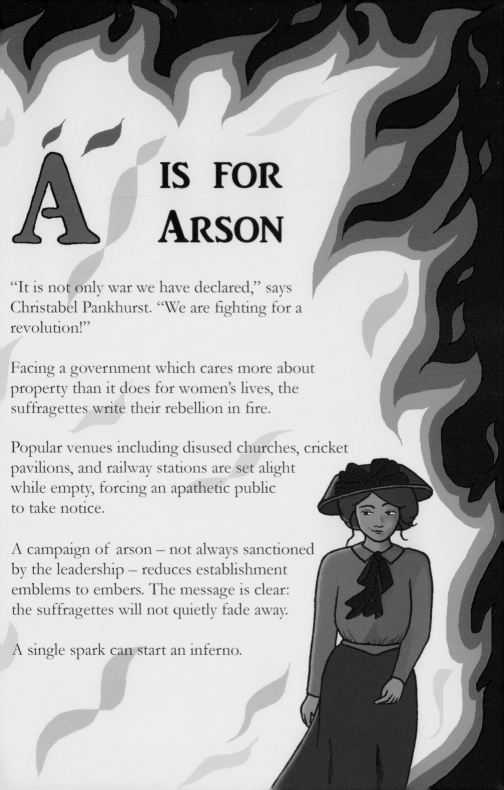

B IS FOR BOMBING

Attempting to ignite the nation's attention – and the establishment's fear – the suffragettes choose key locations for bombing.

Targets like the Coronation chair at Westminster and the Chancellor's uninhabited house see explosive results. Literally.

Even unsuccessful attacks, like one on St Pauls, generate further fear and unrest. The outcome? Headlines, widespread attention, and a hefty repair bill for one of the government's top windbags.

To quote Christabel Pankhurst: "Why should a woman not make use of the same weapons as men?"

C IS FOR CENSUS BOYCOTT

"If women don't count, neither shall they be counted."
Laurence and Clemence Housman thus orchestrate a
nationwide boycott, urging women across the UK to
reject the 1911 census.

Some refuse to fill in their information, others deface
their forms with messages such as "No vote, no census".
Many choose to hide from census officials at all-night
census-dodging parties. Refreshments, card games, and
revolution… a fine time is had by all.

The award for most daring stunt of the evening goes to:
Emily Wilding Davison. Hiding in a House of Commons
cupboard during the night of the census, she is
therefore able to record
it as her address.

D IS FOR DEMONSTRATIONS

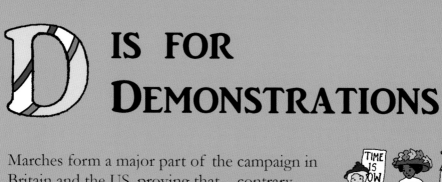

Marches form a major part of the campaign in Britain and the US, proving that — contrary to reporting — the movement has tremendous support. Thousands of suffragettes protest to make their struggle loud, clear and tangible.

Women of all walks of life march and fight for their rights, dressed to impress and adorned with ornate banners and sashes.

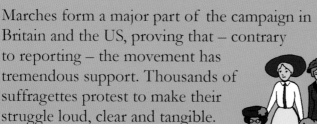

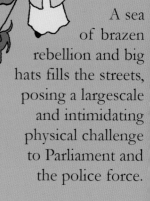

A sea of brazen rebellion and big hats fills the streets, posing a largescale and intimidating physical challenge to Parliament and the police force.

Those who wring their hands and whine about women's suffrage as no more than "gusts and waves of sentiment" (real quote from an MP at the time, overcome with a flight of emotion) see their nightmares come to life.

E IS FOR ESCAPE

When the bobbies come rolling up, itching for a scuffle, it's wise for suffragettes to make a quick getaway. Leaders disappear behind huddles of supporters and the occasional decoy in costume. Many prominent figures in the movement don disguises and pseudonyms to slip under the noses of clueless police officers.

The boldest escape artist of all is one Lillian Lenton. Lillian has a talent for making herself scarce, even in the most trying circumstances. This elusive mouse proves a headache for those surveilling her – when she is eventually placed under house arrest, Lillian dresses as a grocer's boy and simply… walks out of the door, nonchalantly chomping on an apple and reading a comic. She then criss-crosses the country to evade her pursuers, until finally managing to land in France.

Quite the vanishing act.

Decades later, Lillian's obituary in The Times describes her as a "tiny, wily, elusive pimpernel." They can't oppress you if they can't catch you.

F IS FOR FUNDRAISING

Leaflets, venue hire, transportation, nationwide campaigning…
it all costs money.

Artistic suffragettes, including Sylvia Pankhurst, create and sell
limited edition memorabilia to help source funds for the war
chest. Prize items include stationery, badges, jewellery, chocolate,
marmalade, soap, tea sets, and even the suffragettes' very own
board game.

Pank-a-Squith, released in 1909, is won by crossing the board to
enter the Houses of Parliament. Different squares force different
actions. Roll an unlucky number? Those pesky police will send
you back to square one.

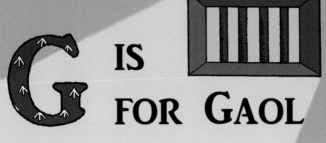

G IS FOR GAOL

Militancy and rebellion come at a cost. Although many of the arrests and punishments only incur a fine, the suffragettes refuse to recognise the court's authority. The result is a gaol sentence.

The squalid, damp conditions feel, as Sylvia Pankhurst notes, more degrading than any pain. Horrendous though it is, incarceration does generate more publicity for the cause.

Even captivity cannot diminish the suffragettes' inherent pluck: composer Ethel Smyth, locked up for window smashing, famously conducts the singing of sister inmates from her cell window, waving her toothbrush as a baton.

H IS FOR HUNGER STRIKE

Marion Wallace Dunlop begins her hunger strike on 5th July 1909. She is protesting against her classification within the prison system: Marion and her fellow campaigners have been assigned the status of common criminals, rather than political prisoners. Others follow suit, refusing all food.

The government grows nervous – anybody dying this way will become a martyr, an icon provoking further outrage among the movement. And so, they enforce a scheme of force-feeding upon all striking inmates.

The procedure is invasive. It is incredibly painful and unrelenting. This practice raises public sympathy in those who see it for what it is: torture.

I IS FOR INTERRUPTIONS

A powerful cry interrupts a political meeting in 1905. The voices are Annie Kenney and Christabel Pankhurst, in the women's suffrage movement's first act of civil disobedience.

Loud and clear, they shout their demand: Votes for Women!

They are ejected from the venue and subsequently arrested. Continued interruptions like these let the campaigners bring their message straight to the lawmakers, in front of an audience.

Naysayers can only plug their ears for so long. There's no pressure like public pressure.

"J IS FOR JIU-JITSU

Over-emotional, prone to impulse, endlessly dramatic… the police never miss a chance to get violent and turn peaceful protests ugly.

Many suffragettes decide to strike back. They learn jiu-jitsu – a martial art that empowers a person of any size to defend themselves against a larger foe.

Under the tutelage of Edith Garrud, a security branch of the WSPU forms to protect fugitive activists from re-arrest.

This thirty-woman group is named the Body Guard, led by Gert Harding.

These "Amazons", as the press dub them, stand with ready hands and clubs hidden in the folds of their skirts to deliver bloody noses to any police officers who threaten their comrades' safety.

 IS FOR KING'S HORSE STUNT

On 4th June 1913, Emily Wilding Davison attends the Epsom Derby. As the horses thunder down the track, Emily rushes under the crowd barrier.

Tragically, she is struck down and dies several days later. It is thought that she wished to throw a suffragette scarf over the King's horse, but her motives are unknown. She acted alone.

The movement is united in grief, heralding Emily as a martyr for the cause. In the aftermath, crowds jeer at her horrific injuries. Queen Alexandra sends a telegram bemoaning the "abominable conduct of a brutal lunatic woman."

Over a century later, Emily Wilding Davison's legacy lives on – a testament to what so many women went through to be treated as full citizens.

L IS FOR LEAFLETTING

Picture the scene: it is London, February 1909. You are walking through the streets.

Suddenly, from the sky, a cascade of leaflets wind their way down across the city.

Look up and you'll see Muriel Matters, in her blimp airship with 'Votes for Women' on the side.

VOTES FOR WOMEN DEMONSTRATION TUESDAY NOV. 2

Leaflets are essentia publicity tools easily distributed an relatively cheap to produce they advertise meetings, rallie processions and event

They are mostly dispensed in a mor grounded fashion, but Muriel's fligh is not the only feat of its kind

Just a year late Margaret Foley follows suit ove a town in Massachusetts, dropping women's suffrage literatur from a hot air balloon

M IS FOR MEN

Not all men throw tantrums at the mere thought of women having the vote. Some step forward and become genuine allies despite pressure and ridicule, recognising the need to educate their less-enlightened peers.

Frederick Pethick-Lawrence uses his wealth and legal expertise to fight for women's suffrage, enduring a prison sentence before eventually reaching high office as an elected MP. Hugh Franklin throws himself into direct action with gusto – even serving time for thwacking a young Winston Churchill with a whip.

As the Men's League for Women's Suffrage say in solidarity: "The petticoat no longer makes the suffragette." "We are suffragettes – suffragettes in trousers."

N IS FOR NETWORK

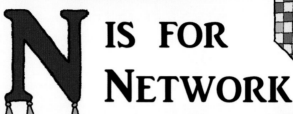

They have the numbers.
The sheer abundance of suffrage
organisations all across the globe is
what gives the movement its power.
Inevitably, activity in the UK
and US, particularly in London and
Washington, draws the most attention.
But freedom has no one fixed location.

The WSPU dispatch key players to
foster a network of activists, stretching
from huge cities to small villages.
Over time, these grow their own
bases of power with individual
banners and slogans. Supporters from
all walks of life swell the crowds. More
and more rise up. The establishment
reaches a nervous realisation.
This storm isn't going to blow over.

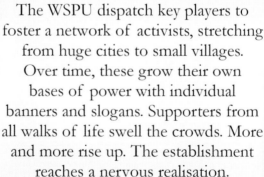

O

IS FOR
ORATORY

"Deeds Not Words" – the famous motto of the WSPU. But words sometimes move mountains.

Talented speakers draw huge crowds of eager supporters, or those tentatively dipping a toe in progressive politics. The women's suffrage movement is replete with firebrand orators, such as Flora Drummond and Mary Gawthorpe in the UK, and Sojourner Truth and Alice Stone in the US.

eployed to different regions, they are the rock stars of their day, sponsible for attracting a vast and committed membership. he usual fools come out in their thousands heckle, of course.

P IS FOR PUBLICITY

No. 2,205.   SATURDAY, NOVEMBER 19, 1910   One Half

It is 18th November 1910. Ada Wright joins other suffragettes to protest in Parliament Square following yet another political betrayal.

A swarm of police confront them.

The Home Secretary, Winston Churchill, has instructed them to dispel the crowd by any means necessary. The police take this literally.

In a riotous and horrifying scene, the police and members of the public inflict disgraceful acts of violence and sexual abuse upon the gathered women.

Many are injured. More are violated. Ada is one of over 200 women attacked in this way.

She is thrown to the ground by the police. Then again. And again.

A photograph Ada, lying bloody beaten, is printed the next day's edit of the Daily Mirror.

The nation wakes to sickening ima and reports of wha now immortalised "Black Friday".

The newspap naturally, are insatia for any chance to up hatred and sm the activists (ev hack's favourite gan

Here, for a chan publicity inspi sympathy for movement.

A light has shone the establishment revealed its brutality.

IS FOR QUEER RELATIONSHIPS

What can be a more potent mix for romance than revolution?

Amongst the hustle and bustle of marches and secret missions, sparks begin to fly – and not just the ones from lit fuses. A heady concoction of danger and adventure combusts into outright desire. Behind closed doors, a number of suffragettes escape the stuffy social restrictions of the era and fall into each other's arms.

Passions are stoked. Relationships form. Many, like Evelina Haverfield and Vera 'Jack' Holme, the Pankhursts' chauffeur, are proud and open about their partnerships. Bound by shared purpose and a giddy freedom from societal norms they are, in private at least, free and deliriously happy.

Decades later, they walk to the polling station and cast their hard-won vote, before returning home to their unions formed in rebellion.

IS FOR RESISTING ARREST

As if trying to outdo one another in pointless arrests, the police take every single opportunity to lock up a protesting suffragette. Peaceful march? Holding a banner? Standing too close? Out come the handcuffs.

Faced with repeated aggression, the suffragettes fight back. Many police officers soon find previously easy collars surprisingly troublesome, or even take an unexpected tumble at the hands of these deceptively unimposing women.

Rosa May Billinghurst goes further, adapting her wheelchair tricycle to become a self-propelled torpedo of righteousness, her oppressors knocked aside like skittle pins.

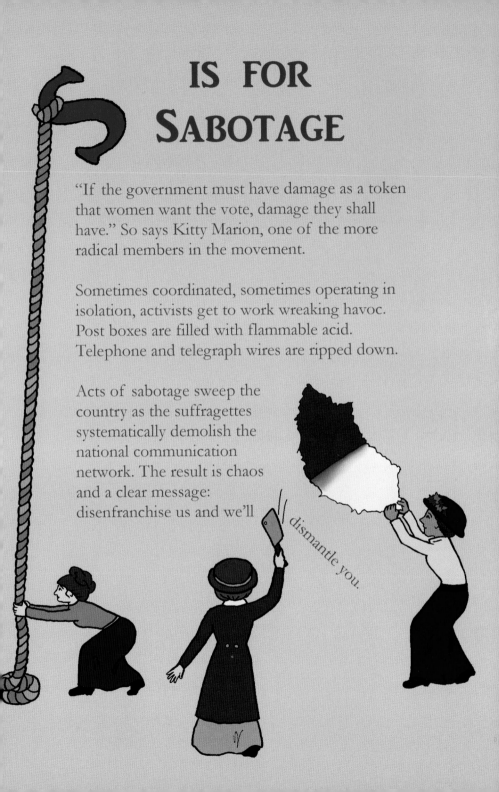

IS FOR
SABOTAGE

"If the government must have damage as a token that women want the vote, damage they shall have." So says Kitty Marion, one of the more radical members in the movement.

Sometimes coordinated, sometimes operating in isolation, activists get to work wreaking havoc. Post boxes are filled with flammable acid. Telephone and telegraph wires are ripped down.

Acts of sabotage sweep the country as the suffragettes systematically demolish the national communication network. The result is chaos and a clear message: disenfranchise us and we'll dismantle you.

T IS FOR TAX EVASION

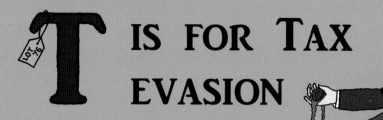

The auction begins. Next lot: the first of two pieces of beautiful jewellery confiscated from wealthy socialite and ardent suffragette Princess Sophia Duleep Singh, a member of the Women's Tax Resistance League. Her items have been seized following her refusal to pay numerous taxes, fines and license fees.

Princess Sophia, in attendance, stands up to address the crowd: "I protest against this sale, seeing it as most unjust to women that they should be compelled to pay unjust taxes, when they have no voice in the government of the country."

The event quickly becomes a fiasco. Attendees refuse to bid, driving the starting price lower and lower until a fellow suffragette buys the lot for a pittance and returns it to Princess Sophia.

By tightening their purse strings and refusing to pay a single penny of their wealth into taxes, affluent suffragettes give the government a real kick in the coffers.

 **U IS FOR UNIFORM**

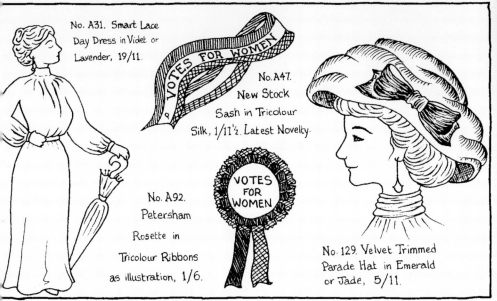

No. A31. Smart Lace Day Dress in Violet or Lavender, 19/11.

VOTES FOR WOMEN

No. A47. New Stock Sash in Tricolour Silk, 1/11½. Latest Novelty.

No. A92. Petersham Rosette in Tricolour Ribbons as illustration, 1/6.

VOTES FOR WOMEN

No. 129. Velvet Trimmed Parade Hat in Emerald or Jade, 5/11.

The women fighting for equal franchise are lampooned in the press and by the public for being man-hating, ugly, slovenly, and not respectable. Sound familiar?

To confound this nonsense, the suffragettes make a point of dressing in smart, elegant, and "feminine" attire, complete with statement hats.

Emmeline Pethick Lawrence develops a colour palette for the WSPU which, unlike that of other organisations, has stood the test of time and become emblematic of the cause.

The suffragettes wear the colours with pride: violet for dignity, white for purity of purpose, and green for hope.

Although there is no single 'suffragette uniform' due to the vast number of organisations in Britain and abroad, they share one common thread: weaponising elegance in their fight for equality.

V

IS FOR
VANDALISM

In 1914, Mary Richardson stands in front of the Rokeby Venus –
one of the most famous paintings in the National Gallery – and
takes out a meat cleaver. One by one, she slashes the painting
with seven sharp swipes before a guard can stop her.

The press dub her "Slasher Mary". Some galleries grow
nervous of further vandalism and bar unaccompanied
women from entry, or even shut their doors altogether.

Mary's act of vandalism, one
of the movement's most
audacious, is a protest
against the treatment of
imprisoned suffragettes. It is
also a particularly
visceral bout of
criticism… she always
hated that painting which
"men gaped at all day long."

W IS FOR WINDOW SMASHING

"Rather broken windows than broken promises."
These words are etched into the handle of several
toffee hammers, which certain suffragettes keep
concealed up their shirt sleeves. When the time is right,
they brandish their hammers and begin smashing.

Protesting against the violence suffered by their comrades in
prison, groups of militant suffragettes leave a trail of shattered
glass in their wake. Coordinated attacks strike private property,
prominent political locations, and major shopping hubs.

Leonora Cohen even takes an iron bar to the cabinet of
crown jewels in the Tower of London.

Many fret about the damage.
They call it uncivil, uncouth,
unladylike. It's a spineless
position. Fix society first,
then worry about
your windows.

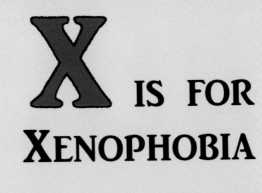

X IS FOR XENOPHOBIA

The suffragettes are brave and unrelenting warriors for their cause. We should, however, not be blind to their faults.

The shameful stain of racism, imperialism and xenophobia exists within the movement, as it does throughout wider society.

In theory, the movement preaches equality. In practice, women of Black and minority ethnic backgrounds are treated with dismissiveness or outright hostility.

Many Brits are openly racist and proud proponents of British imperialism, while white supremacists in the US oppose Black and Native American suffrage.

African American activists like Ida B Wells have to fight on two fronts: against their government, but also against women who should be their allies.

IS FOR YEARS

AND YEARS

AND YEARS...

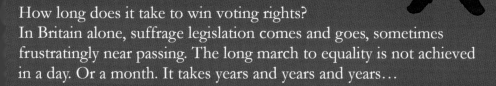

How long does it take to win voting rights?
In Britain alone, suffrage legislation comes and goes, sometimes
frustratingly near passing. The long march to equality is not achieved
in a day. Or a month. It takes years and years and years…

In 1832, voting rights are extended and modernised… but only
to "male persons". Further acts in 1867, 1884, and 1913
extend these further, but again, not to women.

In 1897, 1909, and 1910 a bill granting women the vote passes
the House of Commons… but is disrupted, delayed and
discarded after endless wittering and mind-changing.

In 1913, a new Reform Bill is introduced…
and AGAIN, women are not included.

In 1918, the Representation of the People Act
passes. Women have the vote… but only those
over thirty who have property, a husband with
property, or a university degree.

In 1928, at last, the new Representation of the People
Act grants women the exact same voting rights as men.

Winning equality is not a sprint, it's a marathon.
The fight goes on and on and on.

Z IS FOR ZEAL

A single-minded determination focuses the movement. Its goal is met only after years of sacrifice, violent suppression, and steadfast resolve.

The suffragettes gain momentum and remain resilient following setback after setback. How? Sisterhood. Determination. Zeal.

Progress is won by those who refuse to sit down and accept injustice. Humanity is richer for those who stood – and stand – shoulder to shoulder, taking action to forge a better society from the fire of their struggle.

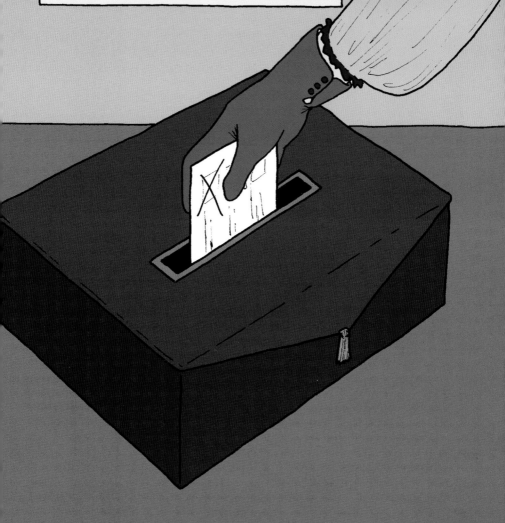

Never Give Up The Fight

**CLAVIS &
CLAUSTRA**

Published 2020 by Clavis & Claustra
5 Lord's Close, Giggleswick, North Yorkshire, BD18 3LX
www.clavisandclaustra.co.uk

Text copyright © 2020 Jack Joslin
Illustrations copyright © 2020 Cat Crossley

ISBN 9780993566844

10 9 8 7 6 5 4 3 2 1

The moral right of Jack Joslin to be
identified as the author and of
Cat Crossley to be identified as
the illustrator of this work has
been asserted in accordance with
the Copyright, Designs and Patents
Act 1988 Sections 77 and 78.

All rights reserved. No part of this
book may be reproduced, transmitted
or stored in an information retrieval
system, in any form or by any means,
graphic, electronic or mechanical,
including photocopying, taping and
recording, without prior written
permission from the publisher.

Printed and bound in England

G000126330

BARBADOS
DIVE GUIDE
BY LUCY AGACE

Published by Miller Publishing Company

All Photography and Text by Lucy Agace
except where indicated

Designed by Eightzeronine Design Associates Inc.

Digital Imaging by Dynamic Colour Imaging

Marketed and Distributed by

Miller Publishing Company
Edgehill, St. Thomas, Barbados, West Indies
Tel: (246) 421-6700 . Fax: (246) 421-6700
Email: miller@caribsurf.com

Copyright 2005 Miller Publishing Company

All rights reserved. No part of this publication may be reproduced or
transmitted in any form or by any means, electronic or mechanical,
including photocopy, recording or any information storage and
retrieval system, without the permission in writing from the publisher.

Printed in Singapore

ISBN - 976 - 95153 - 0 - 2

www.BarbadosBooks.com

TABLE OF CONTENTS

FOREWORD	4	CHURCH POINT	95
BARBADOS	6	DOTTINS	97
GEOLOGY	9	SANDY LANE	101
RECREATION	11	BOMBAS REEF	105
HISTORY	13	FISHERMANS	109
BARBADOS DIVING	15	CRYSTAL COVE	113
NIGHT DIVING	25	VICTOR'S REEF	117
TECHNICAL INFORMATION	27	SS STAVRONIKITA	121
BARBADOS SEA TURTLE PROJECT	29	LORD COMBERMERE	127
SNORKELING	33	CLARKES BANK	131
ATLANTIS SUBMARINE	35	CARLISLE BAY WRECKS	132
OCEAN ADVENTURES	36	THE OLD FORT	139
HAZELL'S WATER WORLD	37	CASTLE BANK	143
BARBADOS DIVE CENTRES	39	FRIARS CRAIG ASTA REEF	147
DIVE SITE MAP	54	PIECES OF EIGHT	151
MAYCOCKS	57	CARIBBEE	154
BRIGHT LEDGE	59	THE BOOT	159
THE PAMIR	63	THE MUFF	163
GREAT LEDGE	67	ST. LAWRENCE REEF	165
THE FARM	71	CLOSE ENCOUNTER / DOVER	169
SPAWNEE	74	HIGH WIRE	173
WHITE GATES	79	CHARLIES MOUNT	177
TROPICANA	83	THE FINGER	181
LONESTAR	87	GRAEME HALL SHALLOW	185
MERLIN BAY	91	INDEX	186

ACKNOWLEDGMENTS

I would like to express my appreciation to a number of people, without whose support and enthusiam this book could not have been completed.
To Mary Pat Rose who put her English Major to good use.
To Susan Duncombe, for the cute turtle photo and being my dive buddy along with Judith Wilcox.
To June Shuffler and Richard Armstrong.
To all the staff and teams at all the dive centres and especially Pete Grannum, Michael Mahy, Willie Hewitt, Haroon Degia, Roger Hurley, George and Sara Sayer.

Lucy Agace with underwater camera equipment

FOREWORD

My love of the world beneath the waves began in the 1970's, not through my own experiences but via the ground breaking underwater documentaries of Jacque Cousteau. Cousteau, the greatest Marine Conservationist and aquatic explorer of the 20th century, inspired the world and left me with no doubt as to where I wanted to go and what I wanted to do.

But life tends to get in the way! I didn't realize my dream until the mid 80's whilst on holiday in Jamaica, when my first dive filled me with awe and wonder and re-awakened the initial interest I had felt almost a decade earlier. After that first experience, I just couldn't wait to explore and to take photographs. I wanted to see everything. It was my initiation into a world I have been fascinated with ever since.

The variety of beautiful, complex and diverse marine creatures never ceases to amaze me, as there seems to be no end to them. I feel the need to capture each marine creature on film, both for my own satisfaction and because I want everyone to be able to see and enjoy this beautiful underwater paradise that exists on our planet. I don't believe it should be seen only by an elite few, everyone should have the chance to appreciate and value this fragile world

What followed that first dive was extensive diving in the Caribbean throughout the next three years and several live-a-board dive boat safaris in the Red Sea. During this time I attempted to master the art of underwater photography, which had become my passion and focus of my diving like so many fellow divers.

My partner and I wanted to extend our diving experiences across the world and, as a result of the fortunate position we were in, we decided to buy our own boat. This would enable us to dive both famous and undiscovered areas, plus explore otherwise inaccessible islands and atolls. Starting in the Caribbean and travelling in a westerly direction the boat went through the Panama Canal and our adventures in the Pacific started. We began with the Galapagos and Cocos Islands, both magical places. Cocos, a well-kept divers' secret at the time, was so amazing that I decided to write a book about it. The book 'Dive Guide to Cocos Island' was published as part of a series of dive guides by Pisces Books in 1997 and is now available via my website: lucy@diving-barbados.com

We spent two years travelling across the Pacific Ocean, visiting the islands of Tonga, the Tuamotu Islands, the Fijian Islands, Western Samoa and Tahiti, Solomon Islands, Truk Lagoon, Pelau and Indonesia. As we moved further west the coloured soft corals multiplied in size and colour, there seemed to be more of everything.

We visited some of the largest atolls in the world and met some amazing tribes people and sea nomads. We explored as much as we could and managed to avoid being lost in paradise!

As the years rolled by so did the oceans and before long we were in the Indian Ocean. Here we first travelled up the east side of Thailand, visiting the fabulous Similan Islands before crossing to the historic Andaman Islands. Six months later we received permission to visit three atolls in the Maldives and then ventured south to the Chagos Archipelago at the same time.

Lastly we returned to an old friend, the Red Sea, and travelled up the entire length in one fabulous seven-week trip, the highlight of which was diving off Port Sudan. It was the end of an epic voyage, one never to be forgotten or repeated.

After publishing the Cocos book, I decided to write about our many experiences on our around-the-world voyage. These adventures are on the verge of being published soon.

My love for Barbados began some years ago and putting together this book has been a huge pleasure and a work of great passion. I will continue to work with the Bajan people to help maintain the condition of their beautiful coral reefs in order to protect their precious inheritance for all future generations.

Lucy Agace

Bottom Bay Beach, St. Philip

BARBADOS

An island of immense charm, natural beauty and character, Barbados has everything to offer holiday makers from all over the world and from all walks of life. Picture the warm sparkle of the Caribbean Sea; 365 days of sunshine each year; and beautiful sandy beaches which can either have every conceivable amusement to offer, or can be tranquil and deserted. Barbados has it all.

The accommodation available ranges from some of the most luxurious hotels and villas in the Caribbean to competitively priced holiday packages and all-inclusive resorts.

Perhaps it is a combination of these factors which has given Barbados the prestigious honour of being the island most visitors return to - over and over again - in the Caribbean.

Barbadians, or 'Bajans" as they affectionately call themselves, are warm and relaxed people who relate well with the constant flow of multicultural and cosmopolitan visitors. From its colonisation in 1627, the island has enjoyed strong links with Britain, and this relationship continues today. In fact, many Barbadians have family living in England and they frequently travel there. There are also strong links with Canada, the United States, and many parts of Europe, and the influence of these countries can easily be seen in many aspects of the island's cultural development.

The rhythm of the sea is at the heart of Barbados, and it plays out in the island's unique brand of Calypso music, served with just the right amount of Barbados rum. Part of the magic of the island is its two distinctly different coasts - the east and the west. The cut-glass western shoreline tantalizes the eye as the crystal-clear ocean gently rolls on to sandy white beaches, canopied by coconut-laden palm trees. This side of the island is calm and protected, and is gently caressed by the Caribbean Sea.

The east coast, however, is quite the opposite, for here the wind rules the waves and creates a pounding surf and a rugged, free-spirited atmosphere which is unequalled anywhere. The Atlantic Ocean dominates the lifestyle of this coast - there are only a few hotels, bars and restaurants, and life in general is slower-paced. The beaches stretch for miles, and a long walk allows the mind and body to soak-up the elements. There is a wave of spirituality that is palpable.

Indeed, these two cultures of east coast and west coast complement each other perfectly, giving the island's natural structure both balance and variety.

Opposite: View of the lush countryside overlooking the East Coast of Barbados.

eft & Below: photos by Andrew Hulsmeier

Cane Arrows

GEOLOGY

Barbados is unique among the Caribbean islands in many ways, and its geological origin also sets it apart. Unlike most of the island chain, the birth of Barbados was not due to a violent volcanic movement. Instead, this coral island - which lies about 100 miles east of the curving string of volcanic islands (called the Windward Islands) - formed over a period of hundreds of thousands of years, and gently rose up from the ocean floor with each successive layer of silt deposit and coral reef formation.

Today dozens of underground streams have carved their way through the island's limestone bedrock and have created a spectacular network of caves. Some of these caves were discovered by the island's colonial settlers in1796, but it was not until 1970 that Ole Sorensen rediscovered some of the central networks and the Barbados Government developed them. Christened Harrison's Cave - as a Mr. Harrison owned the surrounding land - these caves are located in the parish of St. Thomas and have underground pools, tumbling waterfalls, and fabulous stalagmite and stalactite formations.

Opposite: *Lush tropical vegetation*

Barbados is 21 miles long and 14 miles wide and lies in a tropical zone, where temperatures range between 20 C at night and 32 C during the day. Though the Trade Winds offer year-round relief from the hot sun, the Easter (or kite flying) months of March and April are often windy. The hurricane season is from July to October, and affects the entire Caribbean and eastern United States at this time. Though this does not necessarily mean that there will be a hurricane, it does mean that the movement of air and ocean currents converging in the Atlantic may create strong weather disturbances. These can result in systems ranging from clear sunny days to tropical rain to the occasional hurricane.

In the summer months it does seem hotter as the humidity also increases at this time. The seas, however, can often be at their calmest and most tranquil. Sea temperatures at this time can reach 29 C but rarely fall below 24 C in the winter. Underwater visibility is excellent and - because the sea is usually calm - it is possible to dive on the east coast. In fact, I have experienced Barbadian summers with only two days of rain and therefore wonderful diving during the month of August. So, don't be put off by the hurricane season if this is your preferred time of travel.

Although not as lush and green as other Caribbean islands, the gently rolling hills of Barbados provide the perfect environment for sugar cane crops to flourish. The sugar cane

industry was started in the mid 17th century by the English colonisers, and today it remains the island's largest agricultural export. Sugar cane production fuels two economies - the cane sugar is refined into both table sugar as well as into rum, both integral parts of life in Barbados and both equally successful products.

All of the beaches on Barbados are public and easily accessible. The famous Crane Beach on the southeast coast is touted for its soft, pink sand - some of the finest to be found in the Caribbean. There are also dozens of beautiful beaches running along the west coast of the island - many of which are visible from the coast road known as Highway 1. And over on the eastern shore there is the East Coast Beach which runs almost uninterrupted for miles, from Barclays Park southward to Bath.

RECREATION

Barbados is more than just another luxurious island paradise. Besides diving, there is a wide range of activities which include golf, sailing, hiking, polo, tennis, horse racing, cycling, surfing, cricket, off-road rallying, big game fishing, kayaking, submarine trips, visits to wildlife reserves, and of course, shopping.

Top quality golf is available at the Barbados Golf Club, Sandy Lane, and Royal Westmoreland. The Barbados Golf Club was first designed and built in 1974 by noted course architect Col. J. Harris, and was re-opened in 2000 as a 6,700 yard, par 72 world-class facility. The recently renovated Sandy Lane offers two 18-hole golf courses, and the Sandy Lane Hotel itself - with its fine dining, exclusive

villas, and fabulous spa, is often classed as the Caribbean's finest resort. The Royal Westmoreland golf course opened in 1994 and quickly became very popular among locals, villa owners, and holiday makers alike. Set back from the coast and running along an elevated terrace, this course boasts breath-taking views of the western coast and a delightful air of tranquility. There are also two 9-hole courses where non-residents can make arrangements to play; The Rockley Golf Club in Christ Church and The Almond Beach Village in St. Peter.

There are also strong polo and horse racing programmes throughout the year, highlighted by the Sandy Lane Gold Cup held at the Garrison Savannah Race Track each year in early March.

Cricket, however, is the undisputed national sport and is played by persons of all ages all over the island. It is not uncommon to see matches played on make-shift pitches in the road, on the sidewalks, or even on the beach. International test cricket and one day series games are usually played from March to June each year.

My son Max body boarding

Opposite: A catamaran sets off with passengers.

Although people surf all year round on the east coast, in November the sport comes alive with international competitions. Beachfront homes overflow at this time with surfing enthusiasts, all hoping to catch that perfect wave. Still, many others prefer to spend the day playing in the waves, body surfing, or looking for shells and sea creatures in the rock pools when the tide recedes. The east coast, however, is notorious for its strong and dangerous rip tides and currents, so it is advisable to ask where the safe swimming areas are located.

There is a wealth of festivities and festivals held throughout the year. One of the most splendid is called the Crop Over Festival, which kicks off as early as May and ends the first Monday of each August with a massive street parade. It is a celebration of the end of the sugar cane harvesting season and the streets come alive with colourful mascarade bands dancing to lively calypso music. Grand Kadooment Day is a national holiday and the grande finale of the festival. On this day, tens of thousands of people dance their way from the National Stadium down to the Spring Garden Highway, which runs alongside Brighton Beach.

HISTORY

The first settlers of Barbados were the Amerindians who made their journey to the island from South America in dugout canoes. Though relatively little is known about their settlement here in Barbados, several archaeological digs have unearthed fragments of utensils and tools, as well as dwellings and burial sites, and it is believed that some of these date back to around 1600 BC.

Civilisation on Barbados seems to have continued quietly until around 1200 AD when the Arawak Indians who inhabited the island were conquered by the more aggressive Caribs. Indeed, they were the dominant tribe in the Caribbean upon the arrival of the Spanish in 1492. At this time, slavery was forced upon them and new diseases (such as tuberculosis and small pox) were introduced, effectively wiping out their population. Spain's interest in the islands dwindled as they became more involved with their mainland South American prospects, leaving the way open for the English colonisation of Barbados in 1625 - 1644.

Within just a few years, much of the land in Barbados was cleared for the creation of cotton, tobacco and sugar cane plantations which were worked by indentured workers and African slaves. Slavery was abolished in 1834 but almost the entire labouring class continued to live on the plantations and to work in the sugar cane fields and factories. Barbados remained a British colony until 1961 when internal autonomy was granted and full independence followed in 1966. Today, Barbados continues its membership in the British Commonwealth with ties to the monarchy.

Opposite: The excitement of Crop Over Festival climaxes with The Grand Kadooment.
Photo by: Maxie Baldeo

BARBADOS DIVING

Having been a diver for over twenty years, and having covered all of the major oceans and eighty percent of the Caribbean islands, I believe I am well placed to say that the quality of diving in Barbados rivals any other found in the Lesser Antilles. The Lesser Antilles refers to the chain of islands in the eastern Caribbean which is divided into two groups:- the northerly Leeward islands, and the southerly Windward islands. Barbados is located just east of the

Opposite: Schooling blackfin barracuda
Below: Trumpet fish hiding amongst deep sea fans.

Windward island chain, about 100 miles east of St. Vincent

The fact that this dynamic island, the gem of the Caribbean, has escaped the attention of another underwater photographer / writer for many years amazes me. The opportunity was begging to be realized and I can only marvel at my good fortune to be the one to articulate this exceptional adventure. The intention of this dive guide is to ensure that scuba divers get the very best out of their diving experiences in Barbados. Divers can do this by reading the guide beforehand or by using it as a reference while on the island.

As a result of my lengthy experience, I know that every dive can be improved with a little foresight and local knowledge. This is especially true if you are devoted to underwater photography. Many of the diving centres compassionately accommodate photographers and extra help is often at hand to assist with the carrying of equipment. As access to the dive boats is mostly from the beach, any help can greatly enhance the overall diving experience.

Scuba diving destinations worldwide have a range of average, good and fabulous dive sites. What is important is that visiting divers make clear their diving preferences, and that the dive guides do their best to assist them with clear and explicit information.

The diving exprience in Barbados has many attractions. Not only are there flourishing, brightly coloured reefs covered in a variety of hard and soft corals, but there is a superb selection of wrecks - old and new, large and small. They are all complemented by a profusion of beautiful Caribbean reef and pelagic fish. If a reef has a multitude of healthy corals it usually follows that the fish life is equally rich.

Opposite: *Yellow tube sponge cluster*
Below: *This photo of a juvenile trunkfish was taken at night.*

There are rare species of fish such as seahorse and frogfish, along with schools of common reef fish like snappers, yellow goatfish and creole wrasse. Barbados is also home to many large pelagic fish such as barracuda, and various species of jacks, tarpon and mackerel. Sting rays, eagle rays and many eels are common residents, ready to dazzle even the most worldly divers, plus the occasional sightings of manta rays.

Adding vibrancy to the reefs, the orange, yellow, green and purple sponges rival anything that I have seen in the Caribbean islands. Until recently I thought that the Caicos Islands and Dominica displayed the biggest and brightest sponges, but in fact Barbados surpasses them all.

Present year-round, and particularly popular with everyone, are hawksbill turtles. They are common on most dive sites and even venture onto the many wrecks. For instance, there is a resident turtle on the Friar's Craig wreck. Their peak nesting season is between June and September, primarily on beaches on the west and south coasts. As these beautiful creatures are critically endangered due to over exploitation, Barbados in 1998 formed the Barbados Sea Turtle Program (BSTP) and outlawed any harvesting of sea turtles. The BSTP monitors as much turtle nesting activity as possible. Besides the hawksbill species, other turtles which visit the Barbados beaches include the Leatherback and the green turtle.

Barbados is blessed with two distinct barrier reefs and fringing reefs, both of which are ideal for diving. One barrier reef runs parallel to the west coast and the other runs along the south

Opposite: Large sea plume with passing school of creole wrasse.

coast shoreline. Both reefs are separated from the shore by a lagoon which can reach depths of more than 100 feet in some areas. There is also a fringing reef next to the shore in both of these areas. The barrier reefs take the brunt of any passing storms but the inner fringing reefs are still susceptible to surges and swells depending on the seasons and moon cycles. Many of the dive areas on these reefs have an outer and an inner dive site, for such is their depth. In general, both the west and south reefs have similar characteristics, but with some obvious exceptions.

The barrier reef sites tend to vary from a starting depth of 50 - 100 feet. Although the dive centre guides generally only dive down to depths of 80 feet, some of the reefs drop-off to depths greater than 200 feet. Most of these reefs are shaped like an upside down 'U' where the top is 30 - 50 feet across and divers can pick their way along the length of the reef. Though there is plenty to see, it is best also to keep one eye on the open ocean side in case something interesting comes by, like an eagle ray, tarpon or a school of fish.

The inner sites on the fringing reefs tend to be shallow, flat and sandy but are often broken up by large 'islands' of branching or finger coral communities. Soft coral growth such as sea plumes, sea whips and large sponge appear less frequently and there are quite a few up-turned dead coral boulders. However it is here that the rare and smaller species of fish have more frequently been seen. Everything from atlantic squid, frogfish,

sea horses and bright red coral crabs to eagle rays, turtles and tiny flamingo tongue snails have been sighted. These are the calmer, more protected sites and are usually excellent for close-up or macro photography and, of course, for student or novice divers.

Spring, a season beginning in March or April and associated with breeding in the animal kingdom, holds true here. In these months there are more juvenile fish on the reefs in Barbados and, I believe, more fish in general. They come out of hiding to mate and subsequently we can often see more of everything, especially on the shallow fringing reefs near the shore. As with many heavily populated islands, there is some damage to corals on the fringing reefs due to such things as pollution, anchors and spear fishing. However, none of these are a major problem in themselves.

The southern reefs of Barbados are more susceptible to currents of varying strengths that prevail throughout the year. These currents bring the food necessary to sustain the forests of sea fans and gorgonias that populate the reefs. At present these southern reefs only partially belong to a marine park and so the local fishermen generally have a free reign over the amount of fish they catch. Fish is not exported, but instead is sold locally, and there are many 'fish fries' at locations on both the west and south coasts. This is a delightful way to sample local culture and cooking.

The majority of the basket star population inhabit the southern reefs and spend most of the day bundled up in the arms of sea plumes. There are also many crinoids to be found.

Opposite: Two flamingo tongue snails.

Crinoids are members of the echinoderm family and not as common in the Caribbean as they are in the Pacific and Indian Oceans.

While turtles are common on many dive sites on both coasts, a dive site on the south, called The Boot, can boast of being the most likely place to see them. It is almost guaranteed that there will be ten or more.

The undulating barrier reef which runs up the entire length of the west coast is now protected under the umbrella of a marine park. Park rules forbid fishing and as a result the fish populations are indeed greater here. Schools of creole wrasse and boga congregate in mid ocean above many dive sites, and when pelagic fish attack them the schools take evasive action by moving together away from the fish. Atlantic spade fish and jacks are regularly seen flashing across reefs from the direction of the open ocean. Barracudas are also a common site on most dives and it is possible to get quite close.

The further north you travel along the reefs you will notice prolific quantities of many hard corals - star, plate, brain and pillar - interspersed with sea fans and gorgonians. But it is the exceptional diversity of the sponges, especially further north, that sets the west apart from the southern reefs. The sponge growth is greater here and, in some cases, startling in its diversity and colour intensity. The reefs around Speightstown are famous for the beautiful falling arms of the brown octopus sponge, and some barrel sponges have grown so big they are the size of a bath!

Barbados undoubtedly has the best collection of wrecks in the Caribbean. Standing above all others, quite literally, is the SS Stavronikita, a 365 foot long freighter which was sunk on purpose in 1978. She was so skillfully sunk that she lies upright, intact on a sandy bed with her keel resting at 130 feet. This impressive wreck needs 5 or 6 dives to see all of it and is the most often re-dived site in Barbados.

The picturesque Carlisle Bay lies just south of Bridgetown and is the resting place of a group of wrecks that are very easily accessible to both snorkellers and scuba divers. The whole area has recently been made into a marine park and

is one of the few places where divers and snorkellers can access the wrecks from the beach. The Carlisle Bay Marine Park houses six wrecks of varying age and size.

There are two other wrecks that are in fact sister ships, the Pamir, located on the west coast, and the Friar's Craig on the south coast. They were both deliberately sunk for divers in 1985 but the Pamir has faired better, remaining completely intact, while the Friar's Craig has broken into three large mangled pieces. None the less, they both provide excellent man-made reefs, hosting a multitude of marine creatures.

Almost all the dives in Barbados are drift dives, but this does not mean that strong currents prevail. It is merely easier and

Opposite: *The forward mast of the SS Stavronikita.*
Below: *Wreck of the Berwyn with a resident school of snapper.*

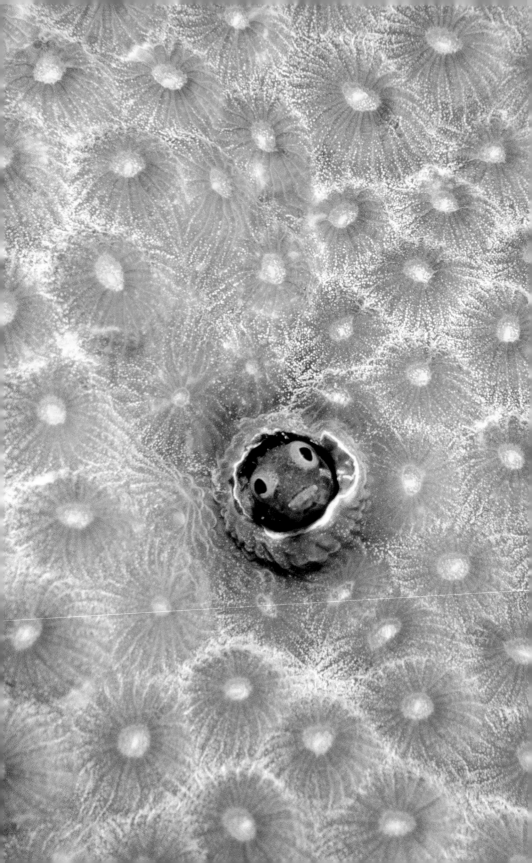

more enjoyable to continue diving in one direction, always seeing a new part of the reef, rather than going back over old ground. There is such a variety of diving experiences on offer in Barbados that any keen scuba diver or underwater photographer should leave the island knowing that their dives have not only been worthwhile but challenging, fascinating, rewarding and, most importantly, enjoyable.

Opposite: A tiny blenny peeping out of some great star coral.
Below: A rock lobster taken on a night dive.

NIGHT DIVING

Night diving is a thrilling addition to any of the day dives you may experience. For those that have never done a night dive before it is not at all scary. On the contrary, the darkness underwater is somehow enveloping, giving a feeling of containment and comfort. Naturally, everyone dives with a torch light that will illuminate a large part of the reef below. Your focus, therefore, is on this lit-up area and the closer you get to the reef the more you will see. You will, as usual, dive with a buddy and there is often

a dive leader in front and one at the rear.

Night diving is a good time to see marine creatures that prefer to come out of the reef under the cover of darkness. For instance, you are more likely to see an octopus at night than during the day. Lobsters, shrimps, crabs, basket stars and crinoids all prefer to feed at night. Fewer fish are out or 'awake' at night, but these fish can be found sleeping among the coral or just stationary and docile.

TECHNICAL INFORMATION

Barbados has its own professional diving organization called the Professional Association of Dive Operators, PADO. This association is dedicated to ensuring the safety standards of local diving and the conservation of the marine ecology of Barbados. Most of the dive sites on the west coast have a PADO buoy which ensures the continued protection of the reefs from anchor damage. Each scuba diving centre is invited to be a supportive member of this programme. PADO is managed and monitored by the Barbados Coast Guard.

It is worth noting that Barbados was one of the first islands to introduce an association for diving safety - the Eastern Caribbean Safe Diving Association (ECSDA). Back in 1984, ECSDA successfully lobbied the government for financial support to supply the island with a recompression chamber that would service Barbados and the Eastern Caribbean chain. The chamber is now owned and funded solely by the Barbados Government Health Services division, and is one of very few in the Caribbean.

The chamber is situated in St. Ann's Fort, the Garrison, just south of Bridgetown. A special health unit of the Barbados Defence Force (BDF) operates the chamber 24 hours a day, 7 days a week. This chamber handles all local diving accidents as well as those from throughout the Caribbean Islands. (By diving accidents I refer to divers that have decompression sickness (DCS) otherwise known as 'the bends'.) This potentially fatal illness is caused when the nitrogen bubbles that form in the blood during a dive are not allowed enough time to escape from the body naturally before surfacing. The reasons for this can include a diver not making a slow enough ascent, or not taking a long enough break between dives, or maybe flying too soon after a dive.

The chamber recreates the underwater pressure which allows the nitrogen bubbles to reduce dramatically in size and pass out of the blood stream. This of course can take a great deal of time depending on the severity of the sickness and may not totally alleviate all symptoms. Providing divers follow the rules they learnt during training, the chances of decompression sickness are remote.

A new 'state of the art' chamber was installed in 2004 and a trained hyperbaric staff member is always in the chamber during any emergency. They work with the worldwide organisation DAN - Divers Alert Network - to make provisions for medical insurance claims. All payments must be completed before patients can leave the island. There is also a considerable charge for the chamber's services - US$375.00 per hour.

It is of vital importance that in any diving emergency, first make direct contact with the chamber and then the ambulance service. The number to call the chamber is: 246 436-5483.

Opposite: *Atlantis Submarine visits Clarke's Reef daily.*

BARBADOS SEA TURTLE PROJECT (BSTP)

DEPT. OF BIOLOGICAL & CHEMICAL SCIENCES
UNIVERSITY OF THE WEST INDIES, CAVE HILL CAMPUS, ST MICHAEL
GENERAL PHONE : (246) 417- 4320 TURTLE HOTLINE: (246) 230- 0142
WEB SITE: www.barbadosseaturtles.org

This program was initialised by Dr Julia Horrocks in 1998 to try and improve the fading number of turtles found around Barbados. Over the past 50 years turtle populations have declined due to over-exploitation by man. Their shells were used for decoration and jewellery, and their meat and eggs for food. In fact, it is estimated that only 1 in 1000 hatchling makes it to adulthood, which takes between 20-30 years. This turtle programme is designed to help turtles safely lay eggs and let the hatchlings make it to sea. The rest is up to mother nature, but at least the human element is removed for the most part.

Three types of turtle visit the island - the hawksbill, green and leatherback. Only the leatherback and hawksbill actually make nests and lay eggs on Barbados. The green turtle is a visitor feeding on sea grasses and algae on the south and east coast. They are in fact quite common in the shallow waters just off of the Lonestar Restaurant beach in St. James, as well as off the coast of the Almond Beach Resort. At both of these places the local glass bottom boat operators

Opposite: A hawksbill turtle resting on the sea bed.

use fish and bread to attract the turtles and it has now become a regular food source for the turtles and a point of entertainment for the tourists.

I would normally be against such unnatural feeding rituals but I have seen many visitors - previously afraid of the water and what lives in it - overcome their fear and get in the water to see the turtles close-up. For those that stay on the boat, they can still see turtles as they are teased closer by food. The experience for them is unforgettable and just may be life changing.

A small number of leatherbacks (the largest of all the sea turtles) nest on the east coast beaches. Females weigh 600-1100 lbs while males can get up to 2200lbs - that's nearly 1000kgs! I would think it takes a great weight to get through the heavy waves on the east side.

Hawksbills are by far the most common turtles here and sightings are daily. It is only when the turtle reaches adulthood that they can begin to reproduce. An adult female will only nest every 2-4 years and between 3-5 times per season. There is a natural instinct within these turtles that brings them back to nest on or near the same beach where they themselves hatched, 20-30 years before. That is why it is so important to keep the beaches free of over development and keep lights down or off at night during the nesting and hatching season. Lights can discourage females from nesting and draw young hatchlings towards the light and away from the sea. If this happens they often die of dehydration or may be eaten by crabs or run over by cars on the road.

The female will dig a nest half a metre deep with her back flippers, up above the high water line. She will lay around 150 leathery, ping-pong ball sized eggs, and this process can take up to an hour or longer. She then covers the nest with sand and, without delay, heads back into the sea. The eggs take between 55-75 days to incubate. After hatching, the baby turtles dig their way up to the surface at night and orientate towards the brightest light, which under natural circumstances is the moon's reflection on the sea. Once in the water the hatchlings will swim out to sea and be picked up by the ocean currents. Here they will spend several years feeding on plankton and floating algae until as small juveniles they return to coastal waters.

BSTP operates a 24 hour call line to report any nesting or hatching activity. The programme is run by the University of the West Indies and most students who attend sites are both knowledgeable and friendly.

Right: Barry weighs the turtle and carries out a check-up to make sure the turtle is healthy.

They enjoy sharing the moment with helpers and encourage children to get involved. The programme is also involved in tagging turtles twice a week. This is

Below: As part of the BSTP Barry Krueger tags and measures a turtle before releasing it back into the sea.

achieved by catching a turtle while scuba diving and bringing it to the boat on the surface. Barry Krueger is the current field manager and usually handles the turtles himself. Any turtle found is taken to the boat and a delicate process of weighing,

measuring, tagging, marking and a general health check-up is carried out. Willie Hewitt from Hightide Water Sports provides equipment and staff to help the programme. Visiting scuba divers are most welcome to join the dive and I would strongly recommend this experience.

Below: *Newly hatched baby hawksbill turtles make their way to the sea.*

SNORKELING

There are excellent snorkelling opportunities in Barbados, for where else can boast seahorses, baby octopus and jaw fish on one beach alone.

As you approach the island by plane, those seated on the left hand side of the plane will see the brilliant white sandy beaches make an almost continuous line up the west coast of the island. Go into the sea anywhere along here and there will almost certainly be something to see. This could range from schools of juvenile snappers, juvenile angel fish, flounders, sergeant major fish, parrotfish and squirrelfish to octopus, harmless eels, jaw fish and starfish. Naturally

Opposite: *One of the many glass bottom safari boats available.*
Below: *A juvenile octopus finds a home in a discarded plastic cup on Mullin's Beach.*

some are easier to see or find than others, but a helpful hint would be to look around obstacles such as rocks, logs, cements blocks, old reef structures, rope etc. Fish use these odd fixtures as a hiding place or home and often congregate there.

If you are visiting the island for a short time it is recommended to use one of the many safari boats, found on any beach, to aid you. These boats offer 2-3 hour excursions to the various marine parks or to snorkel with turtles.

The west coast has two designated snorkelling areas, both within the Folkestone Marine Park. One is situated in a large buoyed-off area in Holetown, St James just up from the Settlers Beach Hotel. This is clearly sign-posted from the coast road, and the site also

offers a picnic area, beach and information centre. Sadly the reef itself is not very vibrant, although there are many signs of renewed coral growth, and marine life is present but sparse.

The second park was established more recently without a designated beach or centre. It consists of a roped-off area with buoys, situated a short distance from the beach in Holetown by the Chefette Restaurant. There is plenty of parking at the restaurant and It is possible to swim out to this area, though most people get there by using the aforementioned safari boats.

The park has a purposely-sunk barge, which has attracted a wealth of marine life. The whole area is teeming with fish such as chubs, sergeant majors, damselfish, chromis and wrasse. At lower levels in the wreck it is possible to see squirrelfish and snapper and, on the surrounding reef, parrotfish, trumpetfish, butterfly fish, surgeonfish, and smooth trunkfish passing by on their daily quest for food.

For the intrepid snorkeller a daring swim over shallow rocky areas in calm seas can be very rewarding, particularly when encountering small creatures. It is here where the elusive mantis shrimp lurks, a fabulous shrimp and a species found throughout the world, but rarely seen. Also one will find lettuce slugs, starfish, tiny pencil stars and sea urchins.

The main snorkeling area in the south coast is the Carlisle Bay Marine Park. This protected park is much larger than the west coast parks and houses six wrecks. They

Opposite: This snail, without a shell, is a lettuce leaf slug, and was photographed with a macro lens.

have attracted much of the same marine life as the west coast parks with the addition of eels, seahorses and octopus. Three of the wrecks are over 60 ft long.

ATLANTIS SUBMARINE

PHONE: (246) 436 8929
FAX: (246) 436 8828
E-MAIL:
barbadosreservations@atlantissubmarine.com

One of the unique qualities about the extent of the entertainment on offer in Barbados is the Atlantis Submarine. This 65 foot submarine takes 48 passengers down to depths varying between 50 -100 feet in safe, dry luxury! Based in Bridgetown's commercial port in the shallow draught area, a large motored catamaran takes you out to the submarine just outside the port entrance. The submarine ride lasts about 40 minutes and for those that can't dive (for whatever reason) this represents a fabulous opportunity to see a thriving reef covered in corals, fish, turtles and rays. On one ride I was amazed to see a school of 100 jacks, their beautiful silver bodies glistening under the bright lights of the submarine. They came right up close to us - so much so I was not sure who was looking at who.

BARBADOS DIVE GUIDE

BARBADOS DIVE GUIDE

35

Below: A close-up of a seahorse's head.

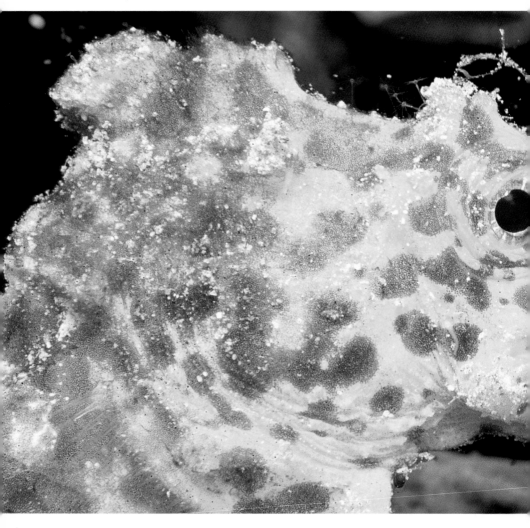

OCEAN ADVENTURES.

WEBSITE: www.oceanadventure.bb

PHONE: (246) 436 2088

FAX (246) 438 3650

Kayaking is usually available at most hotels but for those visitors staying elsewhere there is a company that provides it. Ocean Adventures offer an assortment of exciting tours from sea kayaking, swimming with turtles and snorkelling over reefs and shipwrecks. They have recently added a new activity called Snuba. Snuba is a unique experience which bridges the gap between snorkelling and diving. Snuba diving involves breathing through a 20 foot airline that is attached to a scuba tank mounted on a raft at the surface, which is manned and follows your movement. Snuba is available to anyone over the age of 8

and no previous snorkelling experience is necessary.

HAZELL'S WATER WORLD

Boatyard Complex, Bay St, Bridgetown
PHONE (246) 426 4043
E-MAIL: hwwdivers@sunbeach.net

This is a diver's supply shop that stocks a

good selection of diving and snorkelling gear, for purchase and rental, including children's sizes. Local dealers for Dacor and Mares, Hazell's also offers to service and repair equipment. Other items on sale include t-shirts, swim wear and books.

BARBADOS DIVE CENTRES

Barbados has eight fully equipped independent dive centres scattered along the west and south coasts. They all provide equipment, PADI courses, transport and high safety standards with a friendly service. All centres offer economical dive packages for those that intend to do multiple dives, and prefer the diver to pre-book any dive at least the day before. Most morning dives are two tank dives and leave around 9:00am, returning about 2 1/2 hours later. This gives divers free afternoons to explore the island or go to the beach with their families. Afternoon dives may be anytime after 1:30pm. Times of course vary, and so it is advisable to confirm dive times before booking. A light snack and drink is usually provided, but you can bring your own too.

All the dive centres use aluminium tanks and provide weights for those divers that have their own gear. None of the dive centres in Barbados has a jetty and so access to the dive boats is from the beach.

Starting in the north and tracing down the western coastline, you will encounter the dive shops in this order:- Reefers and Wreckers, Dive Barbados, Hightide, Westside Scuba, Rogers Scuba Shack, Underwater Barbados, Dive Boat Safari, and The Diveshop. Prices for one tank dives including equipment rental vary from US$45.00 to US$65.00. Ten dive packages including equipment rental vary between US$320.00 and US$430.00. Other

Above: A Reefers and Wreckers dive boat
Bottom: Carlisle Bay

packages are sometimes available, and so it is best to approach the individual dive centre directly.

Many of the Dive centres cater for juvenile divers, which usually means children from 11 upwards. There maybe one-off trial dives available as well as Junior PADI courses, which can result in a diving certificate. Junior PADI tends to start from 12 years old but can depend on the childs previous experience and ability in the water.

All Barbados dive centres do their best to enhance environmental awareness. They do not indulge in or condone fish feeding, spear fishing, riding of marine life or collection of shells or coral. Outlined below is a summary of each dive centre giving information on available equipment, boats, dive times and service details.

Apart from the owners some of the diving staff periodically change from one dive centre to another. *"Please bear in mind the prices quoted in this book are correct at time of going to press and they may vary as time passes by. Therefore it is recommended to call and confirm prices with the dive centre before any commitment."*

REEFERS AND WRECKERS
SPEIGHTSTOWN, ST. PETER
PHONE/FAX: (246) 422 5450
PHONE (after hours): (246) 262 6677
WEBSITE: www.diveguide.com

This dive shop is owned and run by Michael Mahy and his brother Philip, Bajans who set up the business in 1993 with their father. Their dive shop is

located in the historic town of Speightstown, less than 1/2 a mile north of Kings Beach Hotel where they used to be. They are PADI certified instructors and offer courses that range from Discover Scuba to Divemaster.

Reefers and Wreckers is the most northerly dive shop, but covers all the west coast, as far down as the SS Stavronikita.

Michael works with two lively Bajan instructors; Archie and Alex. Alex, the boat captain, ensures the boat is in tip-top condition complete with safety equipment and beverages, which are served between dives. Reefers and Wreckers offers a comfortable, friendly environment for their customers to interact with the underwater world and have fun. Divers and equipment are always helped back into the boat without any fuss.

Most mornings they operate a two tank dive - each at a different location, and the first is usually the deepest. They operate two boats: one is 32 feet long with a 400 hp outboard engine that takes a maximum of 14 divers, and the other is 29 feet long with a 170 hp outboard engine that takes 12 divers. Both boats get divers speedily and comfortably to and from the dive sites.

DIVE BARBADOS LTD
ALLEYNES BAY, MOUNT STANDFAST, ST. JAMES
TEL: (246) 422 - 3133
WEBSITE: www.divebarbados.net and
EMAIL: majo@sunbeach.net

Dive Barbados has been owned and managed by John and Mary Moore for the past five years and is situated on one of the island's beaches where there are sighting of

Opposite: A blackedge triplefin fish on a red sponge, photographed at night.

green and hawksbill turtles. This dive operation is geared towards families or small groups, or towards people who would prefer more individual service in an uncrowded boat. John and his team believe diving should be a personal experience and therefore take care in selecting the right dive site for your needs and experience level. John's twin engine 30 foot covered dive boat ensures a comfortable ride to the dive sites.

They have instructors of PADI and BSAC and their courses range from Discover Scuba to Divemaster. Dive Barbados runs a small compressor on site and their shop has a full range of diving equipment available such as Sherwood, Mares and Dacor, plus a variety of cameras. As they plan the dives to suit their customers there are no specific start times to adhere to. John has intimate knowledge of the dive sites all along the west coast from Maycocks to the wreck of the SS. Stavronikita and enjoys leading the dives on most occasions.

Dive Barbados can arrange a dive holiday package complete with accommodation and various water sport activities - further details are available on their website.

HIGHTIDE WATERSPORTS
CORAL REEF CLUB, ST JAMES
PHONE AND FAX: (246) 432-0931
TOLL-FREE: 1-800-513-5763
WEBSITE: www.hightide.com

Hightide Water Sports is located in a new purpose-built chalet in the recently renovated Coral Reef Club in Holetown

Above: *A scuba diver enters the water with a backwards roll.*

and is owned and managed by Willie Hewitt. Hightide has been in operation since 1993 and is contracted to provide the water sports activities for all the Elegant Resort Hotels on the island.

Hightide operates its own compressor and uses Sherwood equipment, which is replaced every two years. It is a busy and successful dive shop and, when necessary, they spread divers between two boats. The smaller one, a 32' mono hull called Flying High, takes 8 divers while the larger boat is a 37' two hull catamaran which will take 12 people. Hightide offers a personal service with

no crowds and can accommodate experienced divers with computers and buddies. There is a 2 tank dive leaving at 9:00am everyday and a single at 2:30pm. They cover dive sites from the SS Stavronikita to Maycocks.

What sets them apart from all the other dive centres is Willies' personal commitment to aiding the Barbados Sea Turtle Project. He does this by giving members of the programme free access to his boat and team twice a week. Every Wednesday and Saturday the first two dives are accompanied by members of the tagging program and everyone is encouraged to look for turtles. Any turtle found is taken to the boat and a delicate process of weighing, measuring, tagging, and marking is carried

West Side Scuba shop & staff

out. Turtles can survive out of the water for up to 1 1/2 hours, but the process usually takes much less than that. If the turtle has already been tagged, then the new information gives an idea of how fast the turtles grow and how much weight they have put on in that time period (i.e, how well they are feeding). This is a fascinating procedure and non-divers are welcome in the boat for a small charge, but this must also be booked in advance to avoid disappointment.

Pam, a full time receptionist, is at hand to answer the phone and help organise the 4 busy instructors, who are Lisa, Edwin, David and Marlin. They offer PADI courses from discover scuba to instructor, with a maximum of 4 people per course. Prices are available at the shop.

WEST SIDE SCUBA CENTRE
BAKU BEACH BAR
HOLETOWN, ST JAMES
PHONE: (246) 432- 2558
WEBSITE: www.westsidescuba.com
and E-MAIL peterg@sunbeach.net

Located right on the beach in the centre of Holetown is Westside Scuba, owned and managed by Peter Grannum and his family. Westside was set up in 1993

43

and is classified as a 5 star training centre offering an extensive range of PADI certified courses. Their expert instructors Peter, Sorren, Tony and Richard offer courses including Discover scuba, Open Water Diver, and Advanced Open Water, and they are one of the few centres that certify up to Instructor level.

There is a professional and friendly atmosphere to this organised centre, where a personal, top rate service is very much in evidence and second to none on the island. After a grand remodelling of the dive shop in early 2004, Westside has a new air-conditioned coffee shop and training centre. Here they also stock a wide selection of snorkelling equipment, single use cameras and t-shirts, while larger cameras and wetsuits are readily available for rent. Westside has their own compressor and use equipment which is regularly maintained and renewed. Pre-arranged transportation can also be made available, and their team will accommodate individual divers' requests whenever possible.

Westside is one of the few dive centres where your tank will already be on the boat when you arrive. Gearing up takes place on the boat as well. If you have heavy equipment or a camera that can't be carried with your gear bag then help is at hand. After the dive Westside staff carry the tanks back to the dive centre and wash the equipment.

Westside has 2 boats - a powerful 34 foot pirogue which takes up to 15 divers and called Jamie Too, and a smaller 32-foot pirogue called Jamie. Both have safety equipment on board and carry a spare diver's kit bag on every outing. An informative dive brief takes place on board before everyone gets their gear on at the dive site. This usually includes useful instructions on currents, dive direction and what to look out for.

Opposite: *Brittle star on red sponge*
Below: *West Side Scuba Centre's boat*

Once in the water any camera equipment is passed on. When the dive is over you do not have to get back in the boat with your tank on, they will take it from you. Between dives they serve beverages and a snack.

Westside Scuba has a daily two tank dive which leaves at 9:00am and the first dive is the deepest. They visit the wreck of the SS Stavronikita once a week and cover the entire west coast from Maycocks to Clarks Reef.

ROGER'S SCUBA SHACK
AT THE BOATYARD, BRIDGETOWN
PHONE : (246) 436 3483 or
after hours: 417 0003
WEBSITE: www.rogers-scubashack.com.bb

Roger Hurley, a jolly accomodating Bajan, manages and owns this dive centre that is based on the south side of Bridgetown in Carlisle Bay at the Boatyard. The Boatyard is a family orientated beach club with beach loungers, children's games and a restaurant. There is a discount on the entrance charge for anyone diving with Roger's Scuba Shack, which is useful if you are travelling with a family who don't dive.

This is a busy, well organized dive shop with helpful and well trained staff who can cater to small groups and individuals. Roger's Scuba Shack's professional service is admirable, and they will organise dives around a client's specific request whenever possible.

Roger and three other trained instructors, teach a range of courses from Discover Scuba to Dive Master and offer many other specialities such as night diver, wreck diver

Opposite: Close-up of a peacock flounder
Right: Emily relaxing on a body board

and underwater naturalist. Ocean Adventures runs their Snuba excursions in partnership with dive shop.

Roger's Scuba Shack runs one major dive boat 36 feet long which takes up to 10 divers. A two tank dive leaves at 9:30am each morning and afternoon dives on the Carlisle Bay wrecks leave around 2:30pm. Soft drinks are served between dives in the morning and the pre-dive talks are well rehearsed and informative. Transport to and from hotels is available and advanced booking is essential.

UNDERWATER BARBADOS
BAY STREET, CARLISLE BAY, ST. MICHAEL
PHONE: (246) 426 0655
WEBSITE:www.underwaterbarbados.com

Michael Young is the owner / manager of the Underwater Barbados dive centre. Michael is a Bajan and has been actively involved in preserving and managing the reefs of Barbados for

many years. His diving philosophy revolves around environmental issues concerning coastal protection and management, and he works closely with the Marine Trust and PADO. Michael and his fellow instructors David and Andrew provide PADI courses ranging from Discover Scuba to Divemaster. They use an air-conditioned room for studying and the beautiful Carlisle Bay for practical work. Michael fills the bottles from his own compressor and uses mainly Sherwood equipment.

Underwater Barbados runs a powerful 31 foot pirogue dive boat and they carry up to ten divers. They operate a two tank morning dive which leaves at 9:00am and also offer afternoon dives to suit all experience levels. Underwater Barbados offer excursions to all the south coast dive sites and north as far as the wreck of the SS Stavronikita on the west coast. The friendly, helpful team take great care to make your diving experience in Barbados a memorable one.

DIVE BOAT SAFARI
GRAND BARBADOS HOTEL
AQUATIC GAP
BAY STREET, ST MICHAEL
PHONE: (246) 427 4350

George is the owner and manager of Dive Boat Safari and was the very first PADI instructor on Barbados. With over 25 years diving experience this relaxed Bajan continues to enjoy leading the dives and courses himself. The PADI courses offered go as high as Divemaster and training takes place in the Grand Barbados Hotel pool. His thirty foot covered pirogue carries 12 divers and he visits

Opposite: A macro shot of a christmas tree worm.

sites from the SS. Stavronikita on the west coast to St Lawrence Gap on the south.

George works with a variety of scuba equipment and fills his own bottles from a compressor in the shop. Oshell the receptionist runs the shop when George, Roger and Derrick are away diving. The first dive leaves at 10:00am but it is advisable to arrive 1/2 hour before to get gear arranged. The second dive leaves at 12:00 midday and the afternoon one goes at 2:00pm, which is usually on the Carlisle Bay wrecks.

Dive Boat Safari can offer wetsuit rentals but they have no cameras at this time. It is of paramount importance to George that every diver enjoys the underwater environment in a relaxed atmosphere. To this end he makes sure all divers are well briefed and comfortable with their equipment. There is no rush to enter the water and his steady guidance down to the reef is calming and stress-free.

THE DIVE SHOP LTD
PEBBLES BEACH, AQUATIC GAP
BAY STREET, ST. MICHAEL
PHONE: (246) 426 9947
TOLL FREE FROM USA : 1-888-898-3483
or CANADA: 1-888-575-3483
FAX : (246) 436 1531
WEBSITE: www.divebds.com

This is the longest established dive shop in Barbados, founded in 1965 by Abdulhai Degia. He pioneered scuba diving in the island, founded the Eastern Caribbean Safe Diving Association and raised funds for the island's recompression chamber. When

The staff of The Dive Shop and George
from Dive Boat Safari.

Abdulhai died in 1992 his son Haroon took
over the dive operation and has continued his
father's traditions.

Growing up on the island, Haroon has a
wealth of experience regarding its reefs and
dive sites, which he has passed on to his well
trained staff. Brian and Julian are instructor and
divemaster respectively, and Charlie and Jack
are boat captains. All staff are well acquainted
with all the south coast dive sites and travel up
the west coast as far as the SS. Stavronikita.
Deena manages the office with confidence

and ease and together they provide an
informal but professional service. Their
equipment is maintained to the highest
possible standard and regularly renewed.

The Dive Shop does not operate a two
tank dive system. Instead the first dive
leaves at 10:00am (deeper between 70 and
90 feet) and the second dive leaves at 12:00
noon on a reef or wreck between 50-60
feet. Late bookings are accommodated
whenever possible (especially if they don't
need a pick-up) but advanced booking is
recommended. Discover scuba courses start
at 1:00pm and an afternoon dive, usually

Sharptail eels can be found out on the reef and on the sand in shallow waters.

on the Carlisle Bay wrecks, leaves at 2:00pm. They are both PADI and NAUI dive certifiers and The Dive Shop is also an ACUC training centre.

Located on the beautiful beach of the Grand Barbados Hotel, this is an ideal location for divers accompanied by family. On Tuesdays and Thursdays there is a morning trip to snorkel with the turtles up the west coast, so call for availability.

ONE ON ONE

PRIVATE DIVE SERVICE
PALM BEACH, HASTINGS,
CHRIST CHURCH.
PHONE CELL: (246) 233 5737
WEBSITE: www.one-on-one-scuba.com

Sara Sayer has been diving the reefs of Barbados for twenty years and her enthusiasm and experience are hard to beat.

Whilst she does not have a dive shop, she specializes in providing a private,

personal service. This allows Sara to customize the dives to suit the needs of a diver's experience and requirements. Apart from student divers, all equipment is carried to and from the dive boat eliminating any heavy lifting.

Sara strives to offer the best service possible with safety at all times, and to enhance the environmental awareness of her clients. This may be of particular importance to experienced dive couples who specialise in photography or like to dive at their own pace, especially in the busy winter season.

One On One offers PADI courses limited to the upper level of Divemaster, including specialties such as drift, night and wreck diving, photography and multi level dives. Advanced booking is essential for all dives and dive courses.

A two tank dive leaves at 8:30am and juice is served on the boat between dives. Afternoon and night dives are available. Private dive boat charters are also available.

Opposite: An arrow crab nestles in the arms of a sea anemone.
Below: After a dive 'G' from Rogers Scuba Shack relaxes with some divers on the jetty in Carlisle Bay.

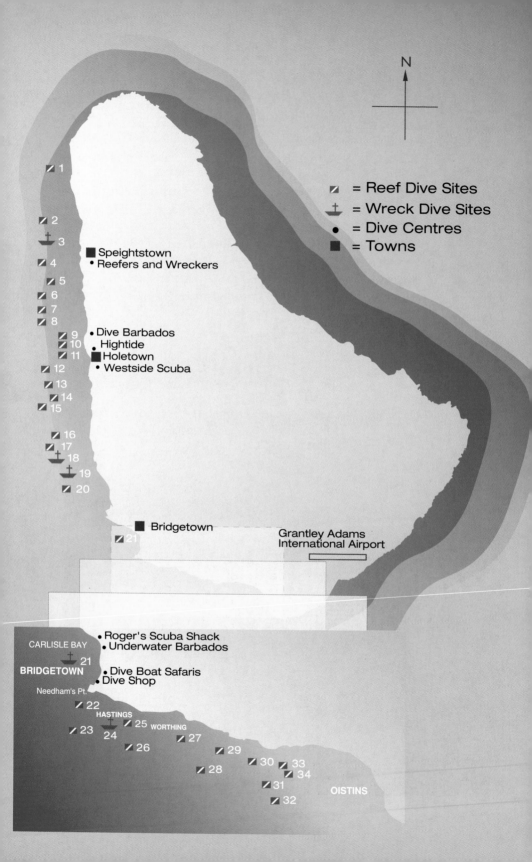

DIVE SITE DETAILS

1 - MAYCOCKS

2 - BRIGHT LEDGE

3 - PAMIR

4 - GREAT LEDGE

5 - THE FARM

6 - SPAWNEE

7 - WHITEGATES

8 - TROPICANA

9 - LONESTAR

10 - MERLIN BAY

11 - CHURCH POINT

12 - DOTTINS NORTH AND SOUTH

13 - SANDY LANE

14 - BOMBAS REEF

15 - FISHERMANS

16 - CRYSTAL COVE

17 - VICTORS REEF

18 - SS STAVRONIKITA

19 - LORD COMBERMERE

20 - CLARKS BANK

21 - CARLISLE BAY WRECKS

22 - OLD FORT

23 - CASTLE BANK

24 - FRIARS CRAIG

25 - PIECES OF EIGHT

26 - CARIBEE

27 - THE BOOT

28 - THE MUFF

29 - ST LAWRENCE REEF

30 - CLOSE ENCOUNTERS/ DOVER

31 - HIGHWIRE

32 - CHARLIES MOUNT

33 - THE FINGER

34 - GRAEME HALL SHALLOWS

BARBADOS DIVE GUIDE

MAYCOCK'S

DIVE TYPE: DRIFT REEF
PHOTO TIP: WIDE ANGLE AND ZOOM.
DEPTH: 50' - 130'
PADO BUOY: NO

This is the most northern established dive site in Barbados and one of the most unusual. Unlike the west coast reef which runs parallel to the coastline, this reef runs perpendicular to the shoreline. This large area of pristine reef is broken-up by a number of deep sand channels, giving the dive a unique quality. Its northerly situation ensures that it is infrequently dived, thus safeguarding the reef's distinct attributes.

Entry is a free descent, down to the reef at 50 feet. During descent have a good look around at the spectacular view of the surrounding reef. The coral growth is prolific with exceptional quantities of plate star coral, brain coral, orange elephant ear sponge, sea plumes, sea fans and gorgonia. In many areas plate star corals have grown to over ten feet in width and some are sprinkled with colourful christmas tree worms. Yellow tube and purple finger sponges are also in abundance.

Because the clarity of the water is excellent

Opposite: Maycock's on the west coast has large areas of plate star coral like the one photographed here.

here, the sand channels give the impression that they are quite shallow when actually they are 100 feet plus. It is advisable to keep a good watch on your depth at all times. These sand channels provide photographers with clear horizontal and diagonal lines to work with and they make a useful background.

There are many species of tropical reef fish, which include hogfish, rock beauties, chromis, coneys and yellow goatfish, but none are abundant.

The reef area is vast, therefore it is advisable to dive at a slow pace whilst looking for interesting marine life close by or on the horizon. Rays, turtles, and eels are regularly seen. A keen eye could even find an elusive green moray eel, but spotted eels are more common. There are many beautiful clusters of branching antler sponge, which resemble the falling fronds of palm trees.

Almost all the dives in Barbados are drift dives which means divers are picked up by the dive boat after the dive.

BRIGHT LEDGE

LOCATION: WEST COAST
DIVE TYPE: DRIFT REEF
·PHOTO TIP: ANY LENS
DEPTH: 60' - 120'
PADO BUOY: YES

This is the second most northern dive site and consequently is blessed with very little reef deterioration. Bright Ledge is part of the fringing reef that runs along the west coast, and the top of the reef is 60 feet deep and about 60 feet across. It is possible to see both edges of the reef drop away. The seaward side has a steep slope (not a wall), reaching down to 150 feet plus, while the inner side shelves to 140 feet. It is possible to dive in a northerly or southerly direction, depending on the direction of the current, and southerly dives will last longer as the reef continues at a depth of 60 feet for much longer.

This is a very popular dive site and gets its name from the spectacular array of brightly coloured corals, sponges and fish life found here. There is yellow, purple, orange and green sponge in all areas of the reef. On close inspection the green finger sponge is covered in tiny bright yellow polyps, called golden zoanthids, which look a bit like mini suns.

Opposite: *A barracuda passes a large orange elephant ear sponge.*

This undulating reef comprises a variety of hard corals balanced with soft corals and sponges, the richness of which is not found anywhere else. It is best to travel across the reef slowly so as not to miss the squirrelfish, lizardfish, rock beauties, hogfish, turtles, parrotfish, whitespot filefish and barracudas, to name just a few of the species you will see.

On one south-bound dive we came across the biggest green moray eel I have ever seen. Its body width was roughly the size of a ten year old boy. Needless to say, I would suggest approaching it with extreme caution if you ever see it! On that memorable occasion I saw two tails under the rock it occupied - assuming they mate, can we look forward to seeing more in the future?

The further south you get you will notice the coral growths seem to get bigger and more concentrated. I often leave this dive reluctantly and wish they could set the buoy in a more southerly position.

Opposite: *This beautiful cascading branching antler sponge is characteristic of the Bright Ledge dive and others.*
Above: *The huge anchor which sits at the bow of the Pamir.* See Overleaf.

THE PAMIR

LOCATION: WEST COAST
DIVE TYPE: WRECK
PHOTO TIP: ANY LENS
DEPTH: 40' - 50'
PADO BUOY: YES

The Pamir is a 170 foot freighter that was modified for diving and then purposely sunk in 1985. She dutifully came to rest upright in a shallow sandy area, perfect for beginner divers and second-tank dives. The bow, which lies at 40 feet, faces the beach while the curved stern is firmly buried in sand in about 50 feet of water. The entire wreck is covered with encrusting sponges of various colours. Black coral and many sea fans have attached themselves to the hull on the port side of the stern. In the central area there is a large open cargo hold where it is possible to see grunts, blackbar soldierfish, trumpet fish, squid and sergeant major fish.

The sergeant major fish are a well known attraction of the wreck, and they provide excellent photographic subjects. The flat surface walls of the wreck are perfect for them to lay their purple egg clusters on, which they seem to do throughout the year. As soon as the eggs are laid the mating pair

Opposite: *There are circles of purple sergeant major eggs all over the wreck and many fish, including this parrotfish, enjoy eating them.*

spends every waking moment protecting their potential offspring from hungry fish, even their own species. If a diver swims too close to a cluster they are liable to receive an aggressive darting attack, so look out! But may I remind you these fish are only 3 inches in length and therefore do not present any real danger.

The hull of the Pamir has many large holes so divers can enter and exit with ease. The internal fittings have been removed so there is very little for diving equipment to snag on.

This is a perfect wreck to 'cut your teeth on' if you have never dived a wreck before, but equally, there is a lot to see and explore for the experienced diver too. The bridge is quite large and open with one surviving window at the front, which is surrounded by pink coloured black coral. And if you are caught short there is a porcelain toilet on the bridge, but sorry, no door!

Because of the large holes in the hull there is plenty of light inside the

wreck, which means there is no need to carry a torch. However a torch light does come in handy if you want to see the true brilliance of the coloured sponges and invertebrates which have taken over the ship.

There is a large winch in the centre of the cargo hold which is home to spiny lobster,

banded coral shrimps, feather dusters, tube worms and an elusive small, white frogfish.

A small school of yellow goatfish hover under the curvature of the bow amongst a scattering of coral heads and barrel sponges. Standing at attention, a huge old-fashioned anchor lies upright in the

Left: *Black coral grows in the bridge of the wreck and one glass window remains intact.*

also see another strange fish called a flying gurnard. They are not often found swimming around but they frequent the sea bed in search of food. These fish are about 12 inches long; they have large eyes and mottled brown backs and are relatively unattractive. However when they extend their wings out they are totally transformed as their six-inch wings are a mesmerizing luminescent blue/green colour.

Popping their heads up from the sand along the port side of the wreck is a colony of garden eels. If approached carefully, crouching on the sand, it is possible to get within a few feet of them.

The surrounding reef is in good condition and supports a multitude of marine life. I found 2 rare red heart urchins, burrowed in the sand. Also there are 4 species of sea anemones, on and around the wreck, and inhabiting them at least 2 species of shrimp - all perfect for macro photography. If you look closely you can find beautiful lettuce leaf slugs and brightly coloured fire worms, crawling across the reef.

At the end of the dive, when it is necessary to do a safety stop at 15 feet, hundreds of brown chromis and blue fusiliers, who inhabit the water above the wreck, come into view. Previously unnoticed, they provide a much needed service by feeding on floating algae and plankton, which inturn improves visibility.

sand at the bow. It is covered by a large multi-angled barrel sponge which, in turn, plays host to shrimp, gobbies and other small reef creatures.

Pelagic fish such as spanish mackerel, barracuda and bar jack can often be seen cruising the wreck and reef area. You may

GREAT LEDGE

LOCATION: WEST COAST
DIVE TYPE: DRIFT REEF
PHOTO TIP: ZOOM, WIDE ANGLE
DEPTH: 55' - 100'
PADO BUOY: YES

Situated just south of Speightstown, this site is similar to Bright Ledge. The reef begins at 50 feet and slopes down quite gently on the seaward side to great depths. While the land side is a steeper slope the water is often murky. The undulating reef top is covered in hard and soft corals. Most notable are the many branching antler sponges. They reach up from the reef like leafless trees.

Visiting this reef is like taking a walk through a garden with red gorgonias, purple sea fans, black coral bushes and sea plumes, all of which resemble the earthly plants and bushes we are accustomed to.

Once again, the dive can be led to the north or south, depending on the current if there is one. A southerly direction is preferable as the reef top stays at a diveable depth for longer.

Opposite: *Yellow tube and lavender sponges stand out on the reef, along with purple sea fans.*
Overleaf: *School of atlantic spade fish are often seen on the Great Ledge Dive.*

There seems to be a lot of fish action here. Hundreds of chromis and creole wrasse swarm the upper waters, constantly on the move. These school of fish look so graceful when, in one sweeping movement, they swerve together to miss the striking attack of a large cero or spanish mackerel. Other pelagic predators include bar jacks and yellow tail snappers. On the edge of the outer reef there is a good chance to see a passing school of atlantic spade fish. This large, round-shaped silver fish with black vertical stripes has a rather shimmering, ghost-like quality as it moves.

Lizardfish, soldierfish, barracuda, scrawled filefish, trumpet fish and scorpion fish can all be found along the dive. Lower down, in between the coral and rock, spotted eels poke their heads out to look for passing food. They are relatively easy to approach but wagging fingers can be intrusive and may resemble food to them, so be careful.

BARBADOS DIVE GUIDE

THE FARM

LOCATION: WEST COAST
DIVE TYPE: CIRCULAR REEF DRIFT
PHOTO TIP: ZOOM AND MACRO
DEPTH: 60' - 80'
PADO BUOY: NO

The Farm is an unusual dive site because the reef is a circular shape. The reef reaches approximately 100 feet across and gently slopes down to 90 feet or more on all sides. Because it is separated from the fringing coastal reef, it often has a current running across it which in turn provides ample food for the abundant marine life. There is no buoy here so the dive begins with a free descent to 50 feet; the highest part of this fairly flat reef.

Covered in hard and soft corals, the reef is home to many fish such as scrawled filefish, damselfish, trunkfish and several varieties of parrotfish. Welcomed visitors at the time of our dive were several yellow snappers, an uncommon pelagic fish.

The Farm is another dive where turtles are likely to be seen. If you find a turtle on the reef take care not to get too close so as not to spook it. Once it takes off don't head straight for it but travel alongside it in the same direction. You may be rewarded when the turtle swims with your group rather than away from it.

Green finger, orange elephant ear, lavender finger and lumpy finger sponge are all common here but what stands out on the reef are the yellow tube sponge clusters.

Large expanses of flat star coral also support a variety of colourful christmas tree worms and there are some lovely ball shaped brain corals.

Opposite: *A small hawksbill turtle takes off across the reef as a diver looks on.*
Overleaf: *This barracuda is using the horizontal arms of a sea plume as camouflage.*

SPAWNEE

LOCATION: WEST COAST
DIVE TYPE: DRIFT REEF
PHOTO TIP: ZOOM OR MID LENS
DEPTH: 50' - 60'
PADO BUOY: NO

Opposite: Yellow goatfish pass over the reef at Spawnee.
Overleaf: It is easy to see why this tube worm is also known as a giant feather duster.

This is a wide reef with a relatively flat top at 50 feet, which gets wider the further north you travel. The reef is covered in an assortment of hard and soft corals but they thin out as you go north. In a more easterly direction finger corals grow in great mountains. They often harbour small fish and crabs. Unfortunately there are a few large areas of dead coral where anchors have landed in past years.

The fish life is diverse and plentiful on this reef, with schools of yellow goatfish, yellow tail snapper, and spotlight and princess parrotfish. It is possible to find blenny fish in the sandy areas; they make their home in a hole in the sand. The hole is only 1-2 centimetres across and is usually recognisable by the small stones laid around the rim.

There are some large yellow tube, barrel and lavender sponges dotting this site, but these are not plentiful.

Large schools of creole wrasse, boga fish and chromis pass overhead throughout the dive. They spend most of the time in the shallow water levels between the surface and reef, but occasionally come down and visit cleaning stations. (Cleaning stations are common reef features throughout the world and a limited number of fish perform the duty. In the Caribbean the bluehead wrasse otherwise known as the 'cleaner' wrasse, a small blue and green fish takes on the task. They get a good meal whilst the other larger fish have parasites removed from their bodies.)

WHITE GATES

LOCATION: WEST COAST
DIVE TYPE: DRIFT REEF
PHOTO TIP: ZOOM AND MID LENS
DEPTH: 55' - 80'
PADO BUOY: YES

This dive site lies between Spawnee and Tropicana on the same west coast barrier reef, and enjoys similar features. The buoy is situated at the north end of the reef so the dive has to go in a southerly direction regardless of the current. The reef is no more than 40 feet across and slopes down the further south you travel. As a result, bottom time becomes shortened. It is perhaps for this reason that White Gates is dived less often than its two neighbours. However, there is still plenty to see so perhaps this dive is best suited to photographers who do not wish to travel great distances on a dive.

There are some very large sponge growths that highlight the reef, along with a few sea fans and good overall coral growth. The reef fish are not as plentiful as the creole wrasse and chromis.

Sand divers, scorpion fish, turtles and eels are around, and on the reef's outer edge atlantic spadefish and tarpon have been seen.

Opposite: *The gills of this red feather duster radiate out like butterfly wings.*
Overleaf: *There is a wonderful array of sea fans and sponges on this dive.*

BARBADOS DIVE GUIDE

TROPICANA

Tropicana is a fringing reef which is part of the reef that runs all the way down the west coast. The top of the reef varies between 50 and 70 feet in depth with drop-offs on either side going down to 130 feet. Divers are not usually led down the sides as the tropical marine life is plentiful on top and deeper diving restricts bottom time. There is often a current, which runs in a northerly or southerly direction, depending on the tides. The dive leader will decide which way to travel on the dive once the current's direction is assessed.

The dive site is named after the abundance of colourful sponges and fish that inhabit the reef. Finding a turtle is more a certainty than a possibility, and spotted eels are common too. Watch out for the elusive scorpionfish; although quite small, the spines on their back deliver a venomous sting. Approach with caution, but don't panic if you see one. They only defend themselves when something attacks them and an inquisitive diver should not constitute an attacker to them. Because they remain motionless, resting on the bottom for reasonably long lengths of time, they can be considered excellent close-up photography material. I found one nestled on a small coral head which produced a wonderful photo. Lizard fish, which are also seen here, have very similar behavioural characteristics but without the venomous spikes.

Dotted around and often seated quite deep into the reef floor are many varieties of anemones. They play host to an assortment of shrimps, including cleaner shrimps and bumblebee shrimp. If you like macro photography they make excellent subjects.

Opposite: *Creole wrasse come down to the reef to visit cleaning stations throughout the day.*
Overleaf: *This shrimp in an anemone is one example of a type of cleaning station, for smaller varieties of fish.*

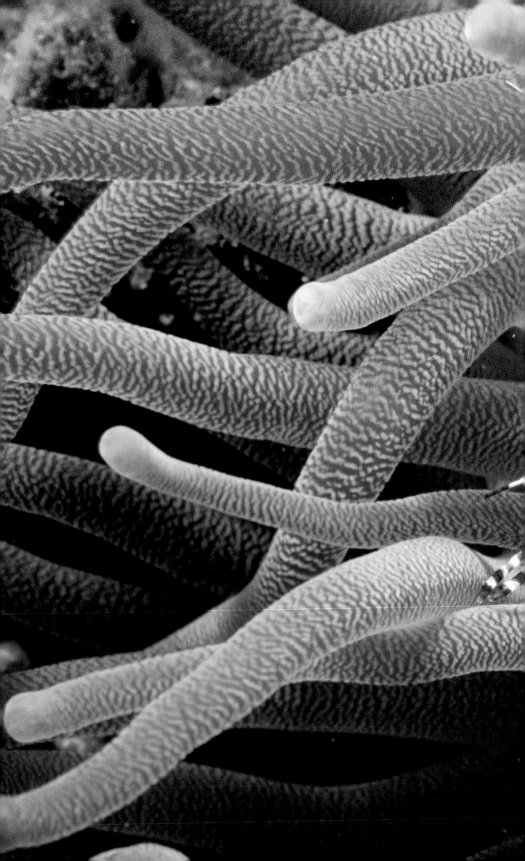

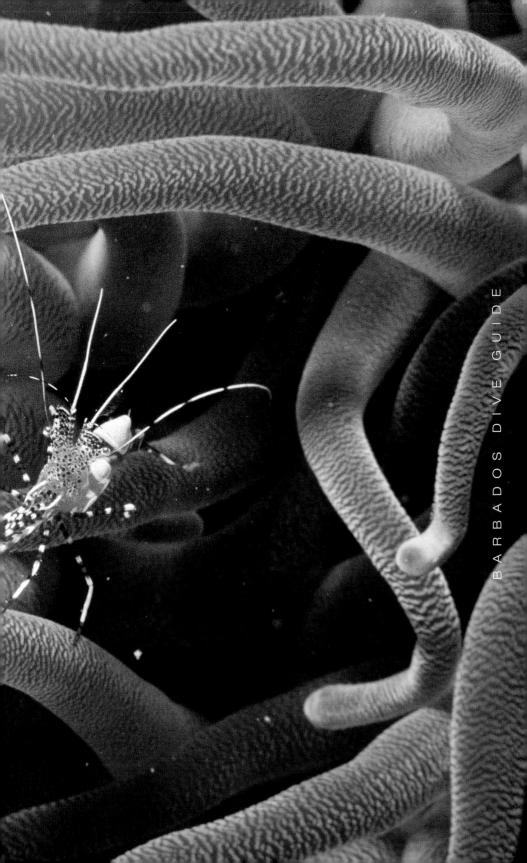

LONESTAR

LOCATION: WEST COAST
DIVE TYPE: DRIFT REEF
PHOTO TIP: ZOOM OR MACRO / CLOSE-UP
DEPTH: 30' - 40'
PADO BUOY: YES

This dive site is situated opposite the restaurant called Lonestar, which lies between Holetown and Speightstown. It is also very near the area where the glass bottom boats bring people to see turtles.

The mooring is in 30 feet on a sandy flat bottom with a number of small coral mounds dotted around. The coral growth gets more abundant as you travel west or north. The location at the beginning of the dive is not very inspiring. It is often used for diver training. But don't despair, the dive progresses north where the reef deepens and a wealth of unusual marine life can be found. Atlantic squid, spotted eels, burfish, pufferfish, large coral crabs, scorpionfish, eagle rays, frogfish and seahorses are all on the reef - you just have to spot them.

A few yellow tube sponges grow intermittently along the sloping reef. They are well worth taking a close look at for it was here

Opposite: This beautiful brown seahorse is only six inches long and was hiding low down on the reef.
Overleaf: This yellow/green frogfish is crouching on an orange tube sponge, using its fishing rod extension to lure prey.

that I found a yellow/green frogfish. This is a very unusual looking fish with a round shaped body and short thick fins used like feet. They sit motionless on the bottom with a transparent fishing rod like appendage sticking up above the mouth. This is to attract unsuspecting food close to its mouth so that it can be gulped down. This beguiling creature is not going to win a beauty contest but he is none the less an amazing sight. I noticed that although he sits in one spot for some time he is very aware of his surroundings.

Feeling elated with the above find, I continued the dive only to see an even more amazing sight. Holding on to a small piece of purple sponge low down on the reef, was a brown seahorse. I infrequently find seahorses, so this was special. I returned twice to search for it but sadly without any success. This was firstly because I had not taken a good enough marker, and secondly because wildlife simply does not stay in one place.

Every time this site is dived something interesting will undoubtedly be seen.

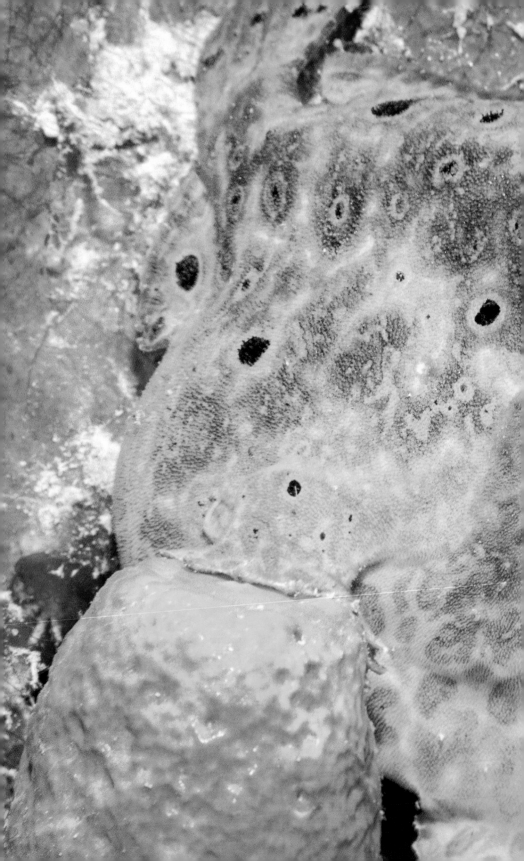

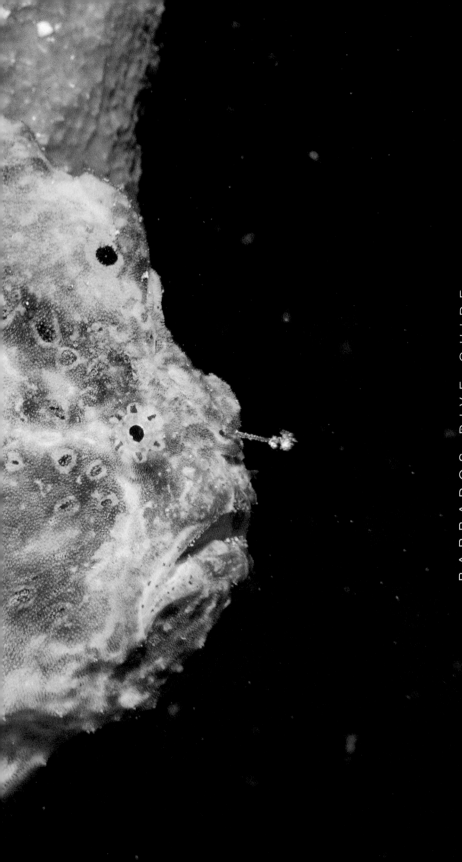

MERLIN BAY

LOCATION: WEST COAST
DIVE TYPE: DRIFT REEF
PHOTO TIP: ZOOM OR MACRO
DEPTH: 30' - 70'
PADO BUOY: NO

This reef is an extension of the Lonestar reef, which is largely covered in long, thick columns of lobed star coral interspersed with sandy areas. With no buoy, this dive site is only accessible to divers capable of making a free descent. The reef is only 25 feet deep at the start and is usually visible from the surface, making descent more achievable. There are a number of large finger coral mountains, a common inner reef characteristic of the west coast.

The reef starts flat and as the dive continues in a southerly direction, begins to slope gently down to 60 feet or more. Here the corals and sponges become less extensive and less sizeable.

It is likely that one will see turtles and sting rays anywhere along the dive, but especially lying on the sand next to or under coral mounds. Amongst the hard and soft corals there is always a chance to see spotted eels and crabs, and the usual tropical reef fish are everywhere. This is a good dive for photography as there are plenty of large sandy areas to settle down on to take photos. Thus making sure no corals are damaged.

Merlin Bay is an excellent dive location for novices and divers that prefer shallow water, but you may need to work hard to search for marine creatures yourself.

Opposite: *Sting rays spend a large part of the day resting on the sand.*
Overleaf: *This close-up of a sea plume arm clearly shows the individual polyps, which look a bit like extended fingers.*

CHURCH POINT

LOCATION: WEST COAST
DIVE TYPE: DRIFT REEF
PHOTO TIP: ZOOM AND CLOSE-UP
DEPTH: 30' - 50'
PADO BUOY: NO

Situated between the dive sites of Dottin's and Merlin Bay, and incorporating many of their characteristics, Church Point is a large pinnacle measuring well over 100 feet across. Church Point, however, does not have the surrounding steep slopes usually associated with pinnacles. Instead the outer edges are flatter and the reef just fizzles out in most sections.

The direction of the dive will depend on the current, for it is possible to dive either way around. As there is currently no buoy, (hopefully that will change in the near future) a free descent is necessary.

The reef's first impressions may be uninspiring but as the dive progresses you will realise there is plenty to see. There are masses of large and small coral growths interspersed with sandy areas. An unusually large yellow tail snapper, which are rare, was seen darting under a mound of mountainous star coral for protection. Sea plumes give height and

Opposite: *Tiny juvenile fish surround a large tube sponge cluster.*

softness to the reef and green finger and yellow sponge adds colour.

There is just about every variety of common reef fish here in plentiful supply, including black durgeon fish - a typical sign of a healthy reef. Scrawled and whitespot filefish, grunts and butterfly fish are easily visible, while moray eels, octopus and turtles are more challenging to find. The large sandy areas attract sting rays and it is possible to get quite close when they are spotted lying on the sand.

This dive site is usually used as a second dive in the morning. For a photographer it would be an ideal time to change to a close-up or macro lens because this type of protected reef allows photographers to find and get close-up to small subjects. In addition, the sand provides a solid base to set down on and not damage the reef. This dive site would also make a perfect spot for a night dive when PADO can successfully attach a buoy.

BARBADOS DIVE GUIDE

DOTTINS

LOCATION: WEST COAST
DIVE TYPE: DRIFT REEF
PHOTO TIP: ZOOM AND CLOSE-UP
DEPTH: 40' - 70'
PADO BUOY: YES 2: SOUTH AND NORTH

Situated opposite Westside scuba dive shop, the south mooring buoy for Dottin's is anchored in 40 feet of water where the rope leads you onto a fairly flat reef that slopes away on the seaward side. There is a north buoy as well which is sometimes called Tall Trees. Currents permitting, it is possible to travel from one buoy to the other on a single dive.

Countless sea plumes and sea whips grow here and in some places it feels like one is floating through an underwater forest of trees. They add an enormous softness to the reef and provide a natural hiding place for trumpet fish and a red fish called the glasseye snapper.

Dottins is not short of fish. If you make a free descent then it is possible you will pass through large schools of blue and brown chromis feeding on the passing food. There are plenty of scrawled

Opposite: Sea plumes like this one are a prominent feature of this dive site.

filefish, peacock flounder, trumpet fish, parrotfish, and barracuda, clown wrasse, threespot damselfish and, with a keen eye, spotted drums and mantis shrimp can be seen. You may also see the whitespotted filefish. Although actually an orange colour, this fish is named for the white spots it shows when agitated or aggravated. One of many beautiful highlights at Dottins is a pair of french angelfish gracefully moving over the reef stopping occasionally to feed.

On one visit to this dive site I saw something wonderfully rare - a large silver flash caught my eye, which I at first thought was a shark. However, I soon realised it was a 5 foot tarpon skirting the lower reef about 60' below me. Surrounding him, keeping up with his every move, were 6 or 7 large bar jacks looking like a police escort! Tarpon are rarely seen during the day as they are night feeders.

Opposite: *A whitespotted filefish takes an upside down position on the reef, which it may do if it feels threatened.*

Dottins is a thriving, healthy reef that has very little damaged or dead coral to spoil the visual impression. Yellow tube sponge and purple finger sponge add vibrant colour to the reef. Some huge towering barrel sponge structures stand out, which give a welcome refuge to small fish and banded coral shrimp. As this dive progressed I felt all the stresses of the day slipping away.

SANDY LANE

LOCATION: WEST COAST
DIVE TYPE: DRIFT REEF
PHOTO TIP: ZOOM AND WIDE ANGLE
DEPTH: 40' - 90'
PADO BUOY: YES

This dive site is located on the barrier reef opposite the beautiful bay where the famous Sandy Lane Hotel stands in Holetown. The mooring line is tied to the top of the reef at a depth of 60 feet and the dive can travel to the north or south. The direction of the dive will depend on the current, which is only assessable when at the mooring. The reef deepens as you travel south while the north gets shallower between 40 and 50 feet. Similar to most of the barrier reef sites it is dome shaped with fairly abrupt slopes on both sides. The outer edge goes down to below 100 feet where the corals give way to sand.

Descending the line will almost certainly take you through clouds of boga and creole wrasse. Together they almost form a barrier before you can see the reef. The reef top is undulating where sea plumes, gorgonia, sea fans and tall sponge clusters stand out. This growth density makes it difficult to set down to take photographs. Add to this the position of the sun directly overhead and it becomes quite impossible to take wide angle shots of the reef with the sun in - unless, of course, you can dive up-sided down!

Both north and south directions have a generous selection of reef fish with the added interest of a seahorse to the north. But of course they don't remain in the same place forever! Pelagic fish such as bar jacks and mackerel pass along the dive usually along the outer edge and barracuda, in small groups or on their own, can be seen. The overall impression is one of activity and colour, for there's never a dull moment. Oh, and watch out for a large green moray eel.

There is a Sandy Lane inner dive but it is rarely visited due to other shallow dives nearby being more rewarding.

Opposite: *A spotted moray pokes its head out of a hole and poses for the camera.*
Overleaf: *Close-up of a french angel fish.*

BOMBAS REEF

LOCATION: WEST COAST
DIVE TYPE: DRIFT REEF
PHOTO TIP: CLOSE-UP, MACRO AND ZOOM
DEPTH: 30' - 60'
PADO BUOY: YES

This reef is located off Paynes Bay and was named after the Bombas Beach Bar which has been recently renamed True Blue. The mooring line brings you onto a flat sandy area at 30 feet scattered with small rock and coral boulders. The whole area is a mixture of broken coral, sand and healthy hard and soft corals. Moving west the reef gently slopes away where coral growth increases and barrel sponges and gorgonias are common.

Several large pillar coral colonies, which are not common in Barbados, are scattered throughout the dive. For a hard coral they have particularly long polyp tentacles. Take a close look at the tentacles because they are usually out all the time, rather than just at night.

A significant feature of this dive are the ten or more impressive giant cities of branching coral reaching twenty feet across and six feet high. Although some show signs of damage, most likely from wave turbulence and heavy anchors, they are still intact and a wonderful sight to see.

The usual common reef fish, such as parrotfish, hogfish, chromis and squirrelfish can be found, but not in as great a quantity as on some other reefs. There is, however, plenty of feather dusters - a type of tube worm which is a good photographic subject. They vary in size and colour.

The area is known for eagle rays, turtles, spotted eels, spiny lobsters and snake eels. Lower down on the reef one may look out for anemones, which often have tiny shrimp inside, or arrow crabs.

Opposite: *Ann, a PADI diving instructor, poses next to a large sponge.*

BARBADOS DIVE GUIDE

Opposite: *This is one of the few dives where you can see large pillar coral formations.*
Below: *This spotted snake eel is quite rare and spends most of the time covered in sand, waiting for prey to come near enough to pounce on.*

FISHERMANS

LOCATION: WEST COAST
DIVE TYPE: DRIFT REEF
PHOTO TIP: CLOSE-UP AND ZOOM LENS
DEPTH: 45' - 80'
PADO BUOY: YES

Fisherman's is on the outer reef at Paynes Bay and is a smaller version of Bright Ledge. The reef is a long dome shaped structure about 60 feet across with steep drop-offs on either side. The undulating reef top varies between 45 feet and 55 feet deep and is thickly covered in hard and soft corals with no space at all to set down. The dive can set off in a north or south direction depending on the current.

Large sea fans and gorgonias add a touch of height and colour to the reef and they often attract groups of two or three squirrelfish at their base.

There is an abundance of orange, purple, antler, green and yellow sponges, but none growing particularly large.

Lizardfish, peacock flounders and scorpionfish can be seen resting on the reef waiting for a meal to swim too close. Blackbar soldierfish, squirrelfish and yellow goatfish congregate among the corals. Turtles are frequently seen, often resting on the reef or swimming around.

Chromis and creole wrasse dart around in the water above the reef, and down below scrawled filefish, coneys and grunts add colour to the reef. It is possible to find the more shy creatures lurking in the depths of the coral, for instance spider crabs and arrow crabs.

Opposite: Here a sand diver sits motionless on a brain coral boulder with a tiny goby on his back.
Overleaf: The spider crab is the largest species of crab found here, and measures about twenty-five centimetres across.

CRYSTAL COVE

LOCATION: WEST COAST
DIVE TYPE: DRIFT REEF
PHOTO TIP: MACRO, CLOSE-UP AND ZOOM LENS
DEPTH: 25' - 60'
PADO BUOY: NO

This dive site is situated just off the beach from the Crystal Cove Hotel in St James. The reef is quite flat and is not prone to currents, making it an ideal place to bring novices and students on a diving course. The buoy is moored in shallow water of 25 feet, giving divers plenty of comfort to descend the rope, and the bottom is clearly visible from the surface.

Moving along in a northerly direction from the buoy rope, the reef begins sloping gently downwards out to sea. Many large and small coral boulders are scattered over the seabed, containing a multitude of tiny marine creatures, such as cleaner shrimp, christmas tree worms and pipefish.

At the early stage of this dive, in the flat shallow area, it is possible to see many small groups of french and smallmouth grunts. More often than not they can be seen staying low on the reef using the coral as protection from large predators. As with many of the dives it is common at Crystal Cove to see rock hind, hamlets, squirrelfish, yellow goatfish, striped parrotfish, blue tang, spotted trunkfish and foureye butterfly fish, to name a few.

It is advisable to keep your eyes open and scan in all directions, as many turtles, rays, eels and squid have been regularly spotted on this dive.

The reef is decorated with some large yellow and purple tube sponges that stand erect giving additional height and colour. A number of very large sea plumes sway to the motion of the sea. Among the many soft plume arms trumpet fish are often found -it is one of their favourite hiding places.

As per usual, at the end of the dive everyone is picked-up by the dive boat.

Opposite: *This foureye butterfly fish flutters across the reef looking for food.*
Overleaf: *Here a peppermint goby sits on closed valley brain corral.*

VICTOR'S REEF

LOCATION: WEST COAST
DIVE TYPE: DRIFT REEF
PHOTO TIP: CLOSE-UP AND ZOOM LENS
DEPTH: 50' - 80'
PADO BUOY: YES

This is a dive site that Westside Scuba found and developed themselves. They recently attached an anchor buoy to the site to protect the reef from anchor damage.

The top of the reef starts at 50 feet and slants down quite abruptly on the seaward side to 200 feet. Depending on the direction of the current, the dive leader will go north or south along the reef which runs parallel to the shore. A wealth of hard corals that include star, brain, lettuce and pitted coral, vie for space on the seabed. These corals have mastered survival and there remains little or no space to settle on the bottom to take a photo. There are plenty of giant feather dusters and christmas tree worms growing out of these hard coral boulders.

There are many tall clusters of purple and yellow tube sponge giving the reef depth and colour while the delicate feather-like branches of sea plumes and whips add softness to the overall appearance of the reef.

Opposite: *Hundreds of chromis fish dart around above a large barrel sponge.*

Smallmouth and french grunts swim nervously among the coral heads in small groups. Various species of butterflyfish and parrotfish pass by with more confidence, along with spanish hogfish. Spotlight and princess, the more common of the parrotfish, are often seen and it is actually possible to hear them biting the hard coral - such is the power of their jaws. Squirrelfish and blackbar soldierfish can be found hiding under coral and sometimes above, but they rarely venture far from their chosen 'living spaces'.

The most notable find on this dive has to be a seahorse. Although common throughout Barbados reefs, they are very difficult to find. Here is a tip: seahorses are nearly always close to the seabed, usually with their tail wrapped around a finger sponge or a strand of soft coral. More often than not they are motionless, making them doubly hard to see.

Left: *This tiny yellow and brown seahorse clings to some green finger sponge at Victor's Reef. Seahorses, however, can be found all over Barbados.*

The ultimate wreck dive in Barbados, the SS Stavronikita stands tall and proud as the biggest and best of an excellent selection of coastal ship wrecks. Although a mighty 365 feet long, lying up-right embedded in sand, she is no-longer a thundering giant but a peaceful one hosting marine creatures instead of tons of cargo.

After languishing in port for two years the Barbados Government decided to buy the SS Stavronikita with the intention of turning her into a dive site. First the ship was stripped of all potential hazards such as loose fittings, metal wires and bent metal. This now allows divers to pass through the wreck without getting their equipment caught. On November 22nd 1978 explosive experts were hired to sink her. They positioned the ship at anchor in deep water off the coast and blew huge holes in the hull in several places. The accurate, timely blasts led her to land bolt up-right on the ocean bed with her bow facing the beach, a perfect execution by all accounts.

Lying at a depth between 30 feet and 130 feet it will take several dives to see everything as the Stav - as she is otherwise known - is so big and so deep that it limits bottom time.

The buoy is tied to the forward mast, which comes to within 20 feet of the surface. Most dive operators attach a reserve bottle to the rope in case a diver needs some extra air to finish their safety stop. The mast structure resembles a long legged giant and is encrusted with a variety of colourful sponges and a forest of hydroids - among them branching, feather and slender varieties.

SS STAVRONIKITA

LOCATION: WEST COAST
DIVE TYPE: WRECK
PHOTO TIP: WIDE AND ZOOM
DEPTH: 30' - 130'
PADO BUOY: YES

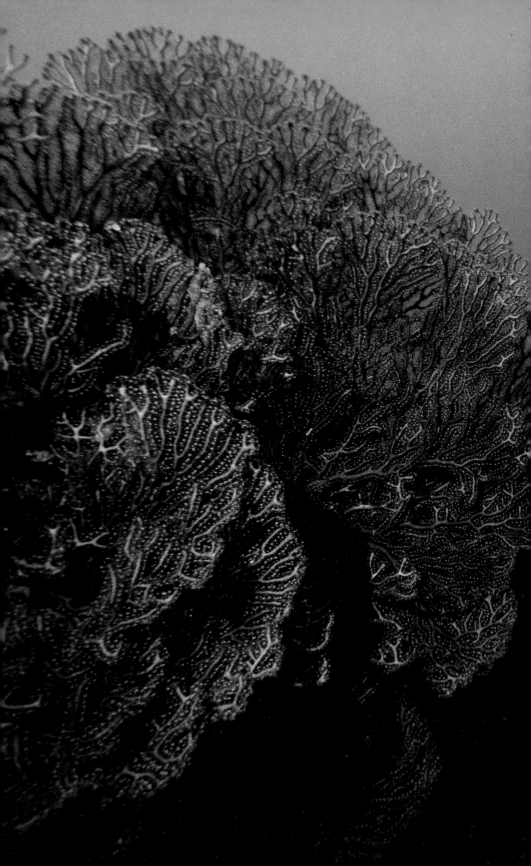

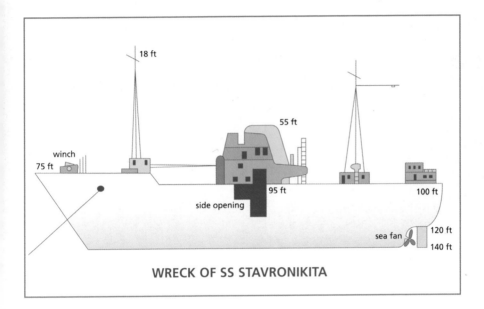

18 ft

55 ft

winch
75 ft

95 ft

side opening

100 ft

sea fan

120 ft

140 ft

WRECK OF SS STAVRONIKITA

On the pre-dive chat you will probably be given the option of taking the deeper internal tour of the wreck, which starts at the prop at 130 feet, or the shallower option, still 95 feet, in the top deck area. For those of you that like the thrill of going deep inside a wreck, speak to the dive leader beforehand as he may be able to take you to the engine room if your group is small enough and experienced enough. There are some very tight holes to pass through to get there but when you see the beam of light shining through, it is truly a unique experience. Massive holes in the hull let in valuable light that penetrates the interior and pieces of hull are strewn on the sea bed below.

Previous page: *A massive anchor chain reaches out of view at a depth of 130 feet, near the rounded stern of the SS Stavronikita.*
Opposite: *A mass of deep sea fans grows on this fallen mid-ship mast.*

In the lower stern area the Stav is covered in encrusting sponges, gorgonias and black coral strands and the rudder and propeller are clearly visible.

There is a large hole on the lower starboard side near the propeller where the deeper internal tour begins. Under the guidance of a dive leader the group is led up through a number of cabins, corridors and compartments to emerge in the cargo hold. There is an alternative dive route - through the upper deck cabins and hatches - and this dive only goes as deep as 100 feet, also ending in the forward cargo hold in front of the bridge. Unfortunately the bridge is no longer accessible due to the fragile condition of this metal structure.

Other places to explore are three large open cargo holds. It is said the bow hold is home to a giant turtle, which I have actually seen. Above the mid-ship hold

123

lies a horizontal beam covered in deep sea gorgonias, which have grown at a diagonal angle to take full advantage of the prevailing current. A large barracuda is often seen around this area.

In 2004 hurricane Ivan caused the bridge super structure to collapse. Consequently it is not recommended to enter the area beneath it because of its instability.

The hull is covered in encrusting sponges of various colours and yellow tube sponges grow in many places. The fish life is not what divers come to see but sargeant major fish are in abundance, they use the flat surface of the hull to lay their egg clusters on. The outer waters are swarming with chromis and creole wrasse. Several species of Jack, chubb and french angelfish can also be seen. The interior harbours blackbar soldierfish, rock beauties, a large green moray eel, grunts and snappers to name a few.

For everyone the end of the dive is spent slowly ascending the huge forward mast. If there happens to be a strong current, there is a long buoy line to hang on to as one decompresses.

Considered an advanced dive by most dive operators, this wreck is well worth a try even if you don't go inside. It is a large wreck and you won't find a bigger one in the Caribbean so don't miss it.

Opposite: This barracuda often hangs around the mid section of the wreck.

LORD COMBERMERE

LOCATION: WEST COAST
DIVE TYPE: WRECK / DRIFT REEF
PHOTO TIP: MEDIUM WIDE ANGLE AND ZOOM
DEPTH: 40' - 55'
PADO BUOY: YES

The Lord Combermere lies a short distance from the mooring line at 60 feet on a flattish sandy area with a sprinkling of small coral boulders. Considering she has been down for 30 years there is surprisingly little coral growth on the hull. Lying up-right and embedded in the sand her rudder is perfectly visible at the stern.

It is possible to enter a cargo hold via a hole in the top deck but there are no other holes and, therefore, no swim through is feasible. The interior does not present much growth or fish life, other than a few glassy sweepers.

After spending perhaps 15 minutes around the wreck the dive leader continues the dive over the adjacent reef.

Opposite: Here a diver rounds the bow of the Lord Combermere.
Right: A golden tail moray eel.
Overleaf: This glasseye snapper is trying to use the sea plume arms to hide in.

This area is not spectacular but sightings of turtles, eels and common reef fish are regular. The reef does feature lavender rope sponge and appears to have a number of cleaning stations and a variety of anemones.

CLARKES BANK

LOCATION: WEST COAST
DIVE TYPE: DRIFT REEF
PHOTO TIP: WIDE ANGLE AND ZOOM
DEPTH: 60' - 130'
PADO BUOY: YES

This is the most southerly of the sites on the west coast reef structure. It is a long boat ride from both of the nearest dive shops and consequently it may have to be requested. Don't be shy or you may miss the best dive on the island.

This is a superb dive, not just because the visibility often exceeds 100 feet, but also seeing the ATLANTIS SUBMARINE is a wonderful thrill in itself. The Atlantis is heard well before it is seen as the hum of her engines is amplified in the water. The expert manoeuvring by the captain of Atlantis allows for ease of movement around her, although it is obviously best to stay where he can see you. It is possible to get quite close and a photo of a fellow diver in the same frame as this majestic machine is not impossible.

If you happen to be visiting the island with non-diving friends consider diving at the same time they are on the submarine. They will be able to see you through the large windows and you may be able to see them too. For the safety of all, divers are advised to contact the Atlantis Operations Manager for information about the submarine and sea conditions and to coordinate dive schedules.

The reef runs out perpendicular to the coastline and often has a current running across it. Because the Atlantis visits this reef no one is allowed to anchor or lay fishing lines or nets. Consequently, the entire reef area is in pristine condition and full of life. Many varieties of hard and soft corals grow in abundance with red gorgonia standing out from the others.

Turtles and rays are a common sight along with schools of horse-eye jacks.

Once again, there is nowhere to set down on the reef as every inch is fought over by corals such as flower, brain and star. Some star coral colonies cover large areas in a single block and there are some huge yellow sponges reaching as high as five feet. There is a feeling of vastness, like being in space, whilst on this dive. Perhaps this is due to the excellent visibility and the enormous width of this barrier reef.

Opposite: *Clarke's Bank is covered in coral like this gorgonia.*

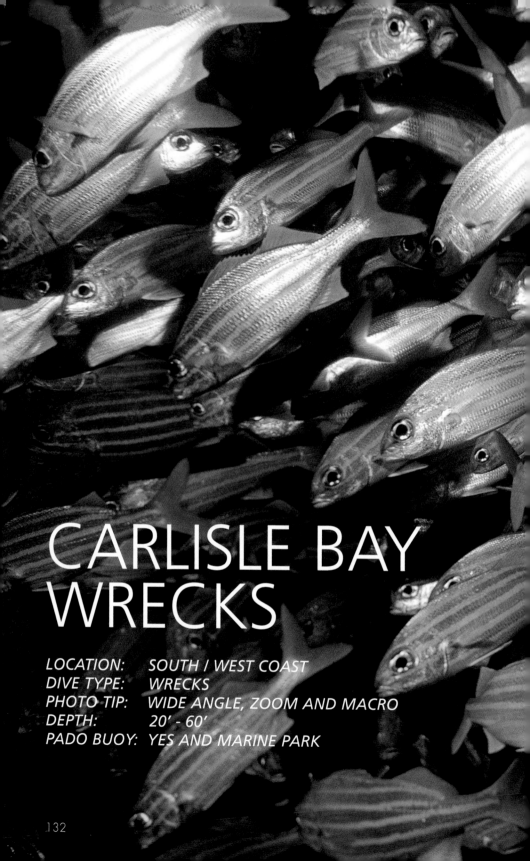

CARLISLE BAY
WRECKS

LOCATION: SOUTH / WEST COAST
DIVE TYPE: WRECKS
PHOTO TIP: WIDE ANGLE, ZOOM AND MACRO
DEPTH: 20' - 60'
PADO BUOY: YES AND MARINE PARK

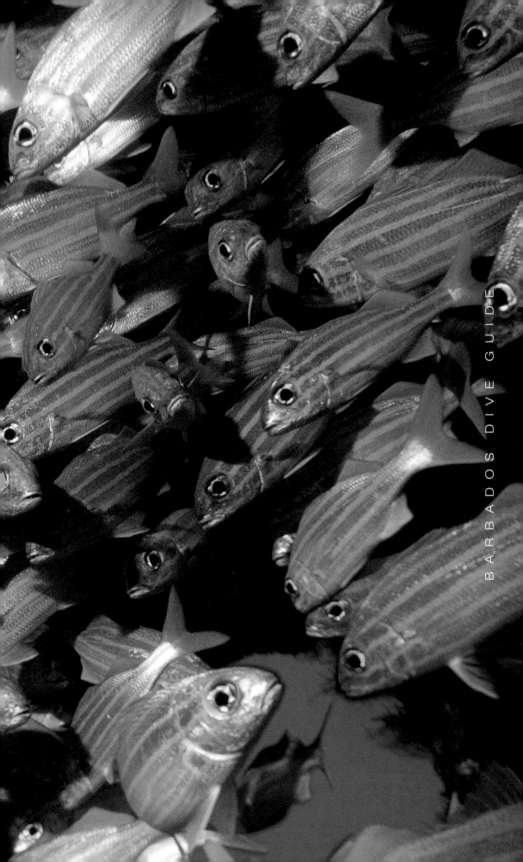

CARLISLE BAY MARINE PARK has an amazing 6 wrecks, all within a small area. This group of wrecks is unique among the Caribbean islands and another great incentive to dive here. It is possible, with the guidance of a good dive leader, to see all 6 wrecks on one dive. Four wrecks were sunk purposely, the most recent one the Bajan Queen in May 2002.

There is something for everyone on this dive site because each wreck is different from the others. Some are big and made of steel while others are small and made of cement, steel or wood. Some have been down since 1919 while others are relative newcomers. They all attract their own distinct marine life, and many wrecks host a variety of fish schools and brightly coloured encrusting sponges. Colonies of multi-coloured christmas tree worms and beautiful pink and lilac finger sponge are also common features.

This marine park is regularly used as a night and afternoon dive venue and is excellent for all aspects of photography.

The BERWYN has a canopy of sergeant major fish at various stages of development: and they shower the first diver that goes near the wreck. Some dive companies do feed fish in this area, as they argue it draws the fish closer to the snorkellers that also visit this marine park. Because the fish come so close there is a good opportunity to get photos of some of the more shy reef fish such as squirrelfish, rock hind, rock beauties, and others.

Previous page: French grunts congregate in an alcove on the Berwyn.
Opposite: Have an early dive on the Ellion and you may find an octopus like this one.

The Berwyn, a 45 foot French tug boat, went down in 1919 and lies in only 25 feet of water. Considering her time spent underwater she is in a remarkable condition and by far the most encrusted wreck. There is one particular encrusting sponge that I have not seen anywhere else - it is small, translucent and mostly dark red in colour.

It is possible to enter the open cargo area and peer through many side port holes, where a schools of small mouthed grunts congregate. If approached slowly they often don't dart off. A large central area is the place where the eels hang out, literally! Spotted moray, chain moray, green moray and goldentails favour one particular spot, where they wait for something tasty to swim by.

Sunk only recently in May 2002 the BAJAN QUEEN is the largest wreck at 120 feet long. Lying in 40 feet of water she is so tall that she almost reaches the surface. The Bajan Queen started life as a tug boat around the 1960's and some ten years later was converted into a 'party boat'. She fell out of commission when bigger and better boats were launched on the party scene. But it is good to know that she has not out-grown her usefulness - as an artificial reef she will live forever.

As she was purposely sunk, the interior has been stripped, and easy entry and exit has been facilitated. On the lower deck, near the bow of the boat, a school of glassy sweepers have

Above: A large group of glassy sweepers hangs out by the spiral staircase on the wreck of the Bajan Queen.

staked-out a home in the doorway by the spiral staircase. They make a terrific challenge for any budding photographer. There is also a large, easily accessible engine room which is inhabited by a remarkable amount of banded coral shrimps. There is a small reef off the stern which is well worth a look, and without much effort I found several anemones, cleaner shrimps and a bristle worm.

CE-TREK was an unwanted 45 foot cement boat left in the port to go to waste. In 1986 the local authorities once again decided to make a discarded boat into an artificial reef. This time they sunk the Ce-Trek near to another wreck and thus the idea of the

Carlisle Bay Marine Park was born. The Ce-Trek has attracted much attention over the years and forms an important part of the park. A large school of yellow goat fish can be found here, often seen with their heads down filtering the sand for food.

The ELLION, a 110 foot freighter, was sunk in 1996 for the purpose of forming an artificial reef. On a morning dive with few other divers I found a large octopus here. Known to be very shy this one was no exception. I followed it as it changed colour several times in the hope of becoming invisible to me, a fantastic display to behold. The Eillon lies on a sand bed at 55 feet and

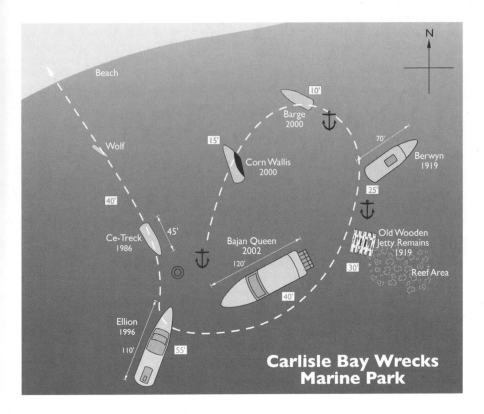

Carlisle Bay Wrecks
Marine Park

is easily accessible for penetration. Not far from here I found a batfish lying motionless on the sandy bottom. After taking 3 photos amazingly it remained completely motionless. Dug into the sand with only the head protruding was a spotted snake eel.

There is nothing much left of the WOLF, a wooden boat dating back to the 1800's - the keel is all that remains. There is a portion that rises up at one end where masses of juvenile grunts congregate for protection in numbers.

The CORNWALLIS was a 60 foot Canadian freighter that was sunk during the Second World War and re-located to this

park in October 2000. This boat lies in a central position quite near to the beach in shallow water of 15 feet. This is an ideal wreck for snorkelling because it is so shallow. There are, however, not as many fish as on other wrecks.

The BARGE is even closer to the beach than the Cornwallis and was once used by the navy. There is not much to say about this wreck largely because it has only been down for 2 years and limited marine life has been attracted to it. A rather flat boat with no penetration, fish such as blackbar soldierfish, Yellow goatfish and snappers use the underside as a refuge.

THE OLD FORT

LOCATION: SOUTH COAST
DIVE TYPE: DRIFT REEF
PHOTO TIP: MACRO, ZOOM
DEPTH: 35' - 70'
PADO BUOY: YES

This flat reef runs straight out from what remains of the historic old fort at the southern end of Carlisle Bay. The sandy seabed is scattered with coral boulders of varying sizes and small clusters of sponges. This is another good dive site for novice divers, as the shallow reef, at 35 feet, is well protected from currents and the reef harbours a variety of marine life.

Close inspection of the boulders can bring rewards, for under one boulder I found a local rarity - a lobster. When I approached to take a photo he even came out of his hiding hole rather than retreat. Luckily for him I wanted to take his picture, not eat him.

The reef fish population is plentiful with many glassy eyes, yellow goatfish, grunts, squirrelfish, chromis and barracuda. A very pretty fish called a spotted drum may be seen here. They look like the zebra of the underwater world, black and white stripes at the front and white spots on the tail end. When juvenile this fish is recognised by an elegant long white dorsal fin that extends the entire length of its body. It flutters about low down in the reef hoping it won't be found.

Christmas tree worms decorate the small hard coral boulders, along with tiny goby fish. There are a number of sea anemones, some with resident cleaner shrimp.

Opposite: Spotted drums spend most of their time hiding under ledges or rocks.
Overleaf: This spiny lobster stayed out of its hole when I approached.

BARBADOS DIVE GUIDE

CASTLE BANK

LOCATION: SOUTH COAST
DIVE TYPE: DRIFT REEF
PHOTO TIP: MID LENGTH, ZOOM
DEPTH: 50' - 120'
PADO BUOY: YES

If there is little or no current here, divers are led around the top of this banking/barrier reef, usually descending down on one side to about 80 feet or so. The dive continues up and along the top area at 60 feet. There is a drop-off, however, on both sides that leads to a depth of over 120 feet. The reef is in good condition and judging by the sea fans and gorgonia facing one way there is usually a generous current running across the reef.

Once again the gentle swaying of the many sea plumes and rods adds tremendous softness to this reef. The ones I spotted harboured not only trumpetfish but also basket stars, which were curled up in the branches. Basket stars are a type of star-fish that have many long spidery arms. At night whilst anchored to something they unravel their arms to catch passing food particles, but during the day they are dormant.

Although short on giant barrel sponge this dive site does have a number of black and orange coloured crinoids, which are rare or absent in other areas. Crinoids are a member of the Echinoderm family, class feather stars. Feathery rays branch out 25cms from a central disc. The arms curl gracefully toward their outer ends and bear tiny tentacular tube feet, which trap plankton from the water. It is usually found at moderate to deep locations on the reef, often attaching to the top of a coral promontory.

At the end of the dive we passed a large fishing pot, which is like a metal wire cage. Unfortunately this one had attracted many fish. But by far the most sickening sight were two dozen spotted moray eels. These creatures are harmless and surely not that good to eat. They are far more valuable on the reef than a passing meal. Fishing like this is legal, but I believe it is time for the Barbados authorities to place restrictions on fishing on known dive sites.

Opposite: *This reef is covered in beautiful sea fans, crinoids and sponge growths.*
Overleaf: *During the day basket stars can often be found wrapped up in the arms of sea plumes.*

BARBADOS DIVE GUIDE

FRIARS CRAIG ASTA REEF

LOCATION: SOUTH COAST
DIVE TYPE: WRECK AND DRIFT REEF
PHOTO TIP: MEDIUM WIDE ANGLE AND ZOOM
DEPTH: 45'
PADO BUOY: NO

The Friar's Craig, a 170 foot freighter, was the sister ship to the Pamir but has not faired as well in her watery grave. Purposely sunk in 1985, she was cleaned of all hazardous fittings and prepared for divers. She lies at 50' feet on a large area of sand about 100 feet across in between two reefs. Unfortunately, she was split into three connected segments by a serious storm.

Lying on her port side she barely resembles a ship at all. If it wasn't for her distinguishable bow, complete with part of a guard rail, she would just look like a mess of mangled metal.

In 2004 hurricane Ivan stripped away much of the coral growth on the wreck.

Opposite: This is the resident hawksbill turtle on the Friar's Craig wreck.
Overleaf: The Friar's Craig is totally encrusted with multi coloured sponges, fans and gorgonia.

Although there is still plenty of gorgonias and sponges on the bow section. Adding to the delightful array of flora are innumerable reef fish, the most notable are squirrelfish, sergeant major, blue tang, grunt, trumpetfish, yellow goatfish and chromis.

It is unlikely that anyone would plan an early morning dive here, but were they to do so they could encounter some rare reef creatures. Wrecks like this one, set in secluded, calm and sandy areas, are an ideal retreat for rays and octopus. If you get the chance to visit the wreck in a small group it would be well worth staying here rather than moving off to the reef. There is a large variety of marine life with good photographic opportunities in easy conditions. Many dive centres talk

about a large resident hawksbill turtle. He is regularly found resting on the sand in the mid-ship area snuggled under an overhang.

The second part of this dive is across the sand to Asta reef which gives the impression of a reef in infancy. Most of the coral growth was in miniature, except for some large odd-shaped barrel sponges. In fact they looked rather like folded-up pizzas standing up-right.

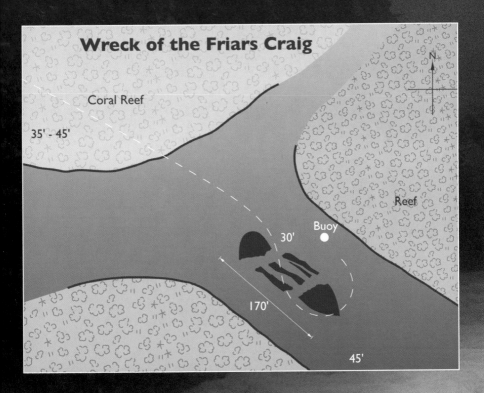

Wreck of the Friars Craig

Coral Reef

35' - 45'

Reef

Buoy

30'

170'

45'

PIECES OF EIGHT

LOCATION: *SOUTH COAST*
DIVE TYPE: *DRIFT REEF*
PHOTO TIP: *ANY LENS*
DEPTH: *25' - 75'*
PADO BUOY: *YES*

Most dive companies on the south coast use this shallow reef as a second dive or afternoon dive. The mooring buoy is anchored at 25 feet on a flat reef, which consists of small hard coral boulders interspersed with sandy areas. The coral is mostly brain coral and many have clusters of christmas tree worms growing on them. From the buoy line the dive continues along the edge of the reef, which gently slopes down to 100 feet on one side. Many reef fish inhabit the small overhanging coral ridges, including peacock flounders with cleaner shrimps cleaning the tiny parasites from their bodies. Other fish action may include a school of sennets - a barracuda-like fish with sleek silvery bodies which reflect the sun's rays as they pass.

After a short distance along the reef stunning mountains of finger coral colonies at least 30' wide by 50'-70' in length, create massive ridges running down the reef. In amongst the hundreds of coral fingers are tiny reef fish, shrimps and crabs that use the coral as a hiding place. On close inspection the small coral fingers are covered in tiny polyps, which during the day may be extended, giving them a fuzzy velvety appearance. This would make a good night dive on a calm evening.

Opposite: Schooling sennet fish dance together in the sunlight.
Overleaf: A group of christmas tree worms.

BARBADOS DIVE GUIDE

151

CARIBBEE

LOCATION: SOUTH COAST
DIVE TYPE: DRIFT REEF
PHOTO TIP: WIDE ANGLE AND ZOOM
DEPTH: 60' - 90'
PADO BUOY: YES

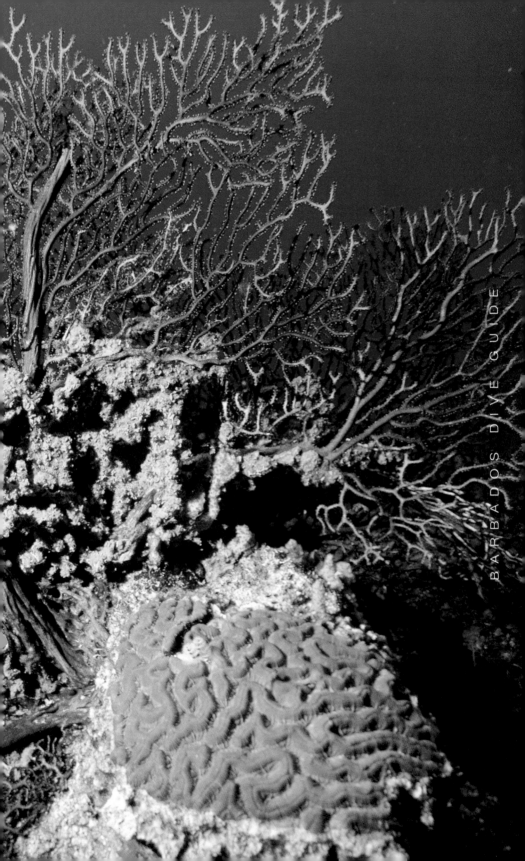

This dive goes in a westerly direction along the south coast barrier reef. The reef is dome shaped with drop-offs on either side going down to 150 feet. It is recommended to stay on top of the reef at a depth of approximately 60 feet, allowing maximum bottom time.

The top of the reef is about 80 feet across and is covered in huge deep red gorgonias, purple sea fans and sea whips. They are all so perfectly spaced along the reef that it looks like they have somehow been planted. They are undoubtedly the main attraction of this dive.

There is the usual sprinkling of fish, but not as many as seen on other dives. At the time of this dive the reef was spawning, and great clouds of tiny eggs covered the reef in a white haze. This is a rare sight on any reef in the world, but I should say it is the second time I have witnessed spawning in Barbados. If you are interested this occurred in November.

As with other areas along the south coast sponge growth is less profound but equally pretty.

Because the reef drops away deeply on both sides it is advisable to watch the edges of the reef for passing marine life. Barracuda, turtles, eagle rays and pelagic fish are all noted visitors.

Previous page: Large deep sea fans are a prolific feature of this dive.
Opposite: This red coral crab has found something to eat in a hole.

THE BOOT

LOCATION: *SOUTH COAST*
DIVE TYPE: *DRIFT REEF*
PHOTO TIP: *MEDIUM WIDE ANGLE OR ZOOM*
DEPTH: *30' - 90'*
PADO BUOY: *YES*

This is a wonderful turtle dive in Barbados, with sightings of green and hawksbill turtles almost guaranteed. In fact, close encounters with these beautiful, peaceful creatures are a regular aspect of this dive.

Descending the buoy line will lead you down to a 30 foot deep sandy area on the edge of a flat reef which is covered in soft sea plumes. These soft gently swaying corals invite you across the reef and bestow a feeling of relaxation.

Among these delicate trees are sandy patches, rocks and large hard coral boulders. From a distance it would be true to say the rocks and boulders look remarkably like a resting turtle. Given an ample supply of their favourite variety of sponge, it is no wonder so many turtles are attracted to this reef. The Boot is a natural safe haven with perfect camouflage and a steady food supply. The turtles vary in size from juvenile to large adult males, some of which even have remoras attached to them.

The reef top is about 30 feet across and the outer edge slopes down at a 35 degree angle to a flat sandy area at 90 feet, where sting rays can be found resting. There are three schooling fish of reasonable numbers: yellow goatfish, horse-eye jack and creole wrasse. Naturally, here as with many other sites, the soft arms of the sea plumes are used by many trumpet fish for concealment.

The dive generally goes across the reef to the outer slope and along to the far end, then turns back along the inside where the reef meets a flat sandy area. Along this edge is another chance to see sting rays and the very skittish atlantic squid. There is no need to go back to the boat as divers are picked up where they surface.

Opposite: *A resting green turtle has two remoras lying on its back.*
Overleaf: *This scene awaits divers of The Boot.*

THE MUFF

LOCATION: SOUTH COAST
DIVE TYPE: DRIFT REEF
PHOTO TIP: WIDE ANGLE OR ZOOM
DEPTH: 70' - 100+'
PADO BUOY: YES

The mooring line on this dive is located at a depth of 70 feet at the top of this long ridge-like reef. The top is about 80 feet across and drops off sharply on the seaward side to more than150 feet, while the other side slopes to a depth of 100 feet. To prolong the length of the dive time it is best to stay on top of the reef rather than venture down the sides. In any case there is a wealth of marine life on the top.

An abundance of huge sea fans, sea plumes and whips and barrel sponges break up the undulating reef, and orange elephant ear sponge adds splashes of bright colour. The large and small brain coral boulders are frequented by lizardfish in particular.

Barracuda and turtles cruise the reef looking for food and a peaceful place to rest. Turtles can stay underwater for up to 1 1/2 hours before having to surface for air, and usually choose soft places to rest, such as where there are large areas of sponge growth. When they are lying still they are very hard to see until you are almost on top of them. They usually see you first and move. This is a good photo opportunity as they take time to get themselves up off the reef because of their cumbersome, heavy shell.

The growth of large cascading brown lumpy finger sponge is prolific here and black bar soldier fish can often be found hiding beneath them. Huge barrel sponges make an impact on the reef and banded coral shrimps are regularly seen inside them.

Opposite: *A V shaped orange / yellow sponge stands out on the reef.*

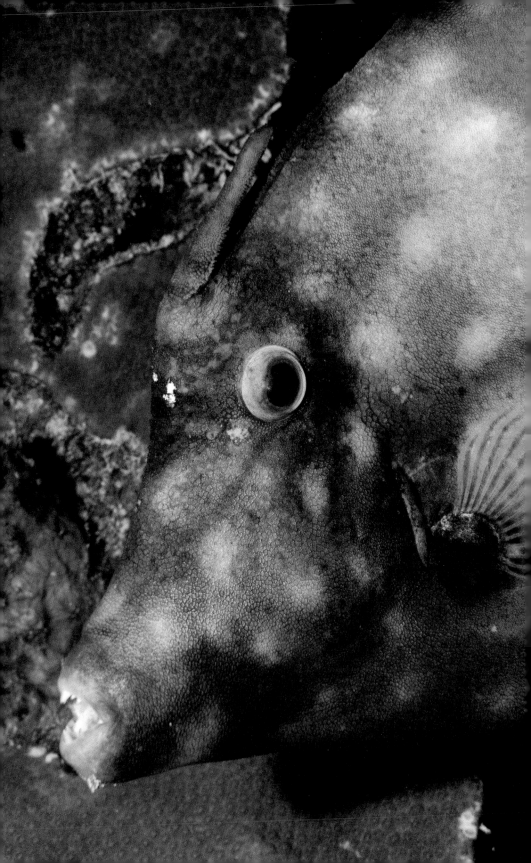

ST. LAWRENCE REEF

LOCATION: SOUTH COAST
DIVE TYPE: SHALLOW DRIFT REEF
PHOTO TIP: CLOSE-UP AND MACRO LENS
DEPTH: 30' - 50'
PADO BUOY: NO

There is no buoy to pin point the start of this dive but you can descend anywhere along this fringing reef. The dive is usually led to the west with the reef on your right shoulder. Unforunately, visibility on this dive can be hindered if the wind is high or if it has just rained.

The top of the reef is at 25 feet and gently slopes down to 45 feet where it meets a bed of sand. This then slopes away over a sand ridge to greater depths. I would encourage that you have a look for sting rays resting on the sand in this area. This would also be a good opportunity to get photos of garden eels because the flat sand bed is shallow and expansive.

The dive guide will take you along the reef's edge where you should look out for turtles, barracuda, octopus and anemones to name the less ordinary subjects.

Nooks and crannies under rock boulders and soft swaying sea plume arms may harbour fish and turtles, so this is not a dive to be rushed.

Opposite: The white spots on a whitespotted filefish only stand out when the fish is alarmed.
Overleaf : This is one of the more unusual anemones found in Barbados.

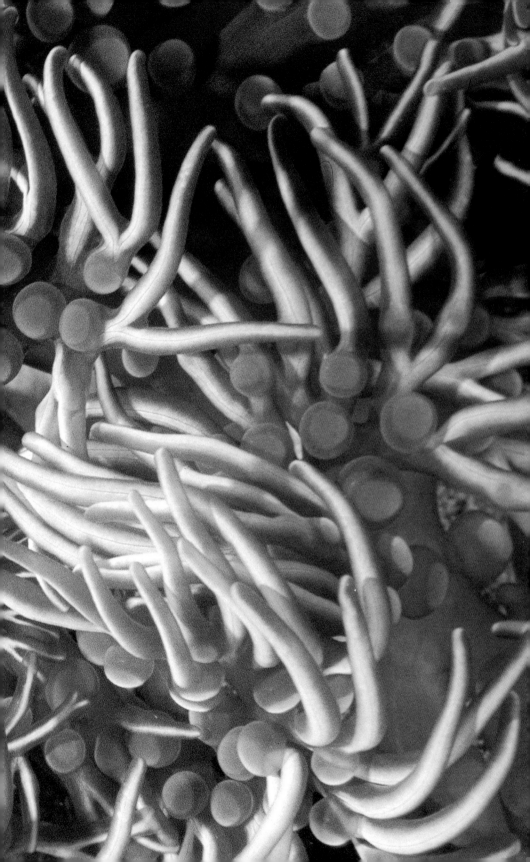

CLOSE ENCOUNTER / DOVER

LOCATION: SOUTH COAST
DIVE TYPE: DRIFT REEF
PHOTO TIP: CLOSE-UP, MACRO AND ZOOM
DEPTH: 30' - 45'
PADO BUOY: NO

This dive site has been given two names so which one is used will depend on which dive centre you are diving with. Located on the shallow fringing reef that runs parallel to the south coast, this dive is just off Dover Beach, hence its second name.

The reef at 30 feet is usually visible from the surface, and following a free descent the dive is led in a westerly direction, keeping the reef on the right shoulder. Diving along the edge, the reef meets the sand at a depth of 45 feet, and here you may encounter turtles and sting rays. The reef edge sweeps in and then out again, so diving in a reasonable straight line will necessitate some travel over sand.

The sand area, however, has quite a few small groups of tiny feather dusters, razorfish and some garden eels. Garden eels are very shy and usually withdraw into their tiny holes whenever something comes near. They are of course worried about predators. Approached

Opposite: Yellow tube sponge entwined with green and pink finger sponge.

very slowly and low down to the sand, they sometimes come back out and will pose quite nicely for the camera. This may take some time though, so watch out that you don't lose the rest of the dive group.

The reef is covered with sea fans and soft gorgonias interspersed with hard corals, rock and small colourful sponges. The bright yellow stripes of smallmouth and french grunts add colour to the reef scene as they shimmer past. Like squirrelfish, they are not loner fish, but instead prefer the safety-in-numbers principle. Trumpet fish are also common, most notably, in their yellow or blue colour phase.

Although this reef is close to the shore a few pelagic fish such as bar jacks and cero pass by, and coloured chromis feed on the plankton above the reef.

For divers or photographers looking for the smaller reef creatures there are a number of purple tipped anemones hosting two types of shrimp.

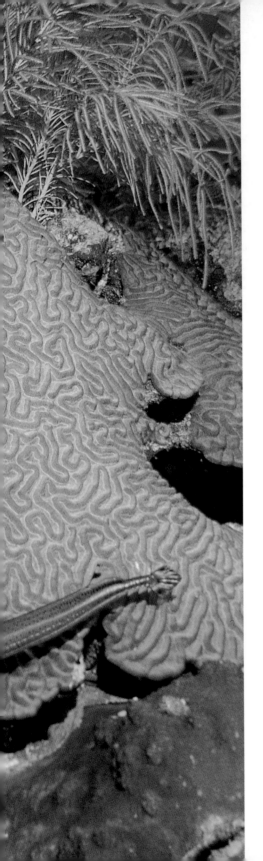

Opposite: *A blue phase trumpet fish passes a large brain coral boulder on the reef.*

171

HIGH WIRE

LOCATION: SOUTH COAST
DIVE TYPE: DRIFT REEF
PHOTO TIP: WIDE ANGLE, MID W/A OR ZOOM
DEPTH: 60' - 100'
PADO BUOY: YES

High Wire is one of the furthest sites along the South coast, near to Oistins Bay, and therefore not always a pleasant journey when the wind is up or the sea is rough. For divers, however, it is well worth the effort.

The buoy is moored in 60 feet on top of a beautiful healthy reef that is covered in hard and soft corals. This site is usually blessed with good visibility because it lies quite a way offshore where currents remove run-off water and provide rich nourishment for the corals. Rather like some of the more northerly dives of the west coast, this reef is very easy on the eye. It is full of colour and marine life and there is a sense of peacefulness here.

The dive can go either to the west or east depending on currents or preferences. It is regarded as a deep first dive because the reef slopes away, quite steeply on one side, to beyond 100 feet. As this is an outer banking reef dive it is best to keep one eye looking out to sea in case something large and interesting goes by. The site gets its name from a large wire cable discarded or lost by a vessel which now is part of the reef.

There is an abundance of large brown sponge clusters along with other coloured sponges. The hard coral formations are principally plate, star and brain. These are complemented by the presence of deep sea fans, sea plumes and sea whips. Some of the lower slopes have huge black coral strands spiralling out like giant cork screws.

The fish life complements the reef and, other than the usual common varieties, the addition of queen angel fish adds brilliance as they dart around. Queen angelfish are very skittish and I would warn against being drawn deeper down to get a closer look.

The upper water area is teeming with boga fish, a small blue/silver fish shaped like a long sausage. Mackerels, jacks and yellow snapper can also be seen passing by.

Opposite: *A beautiful orange elephant ear sponge has become entwined with pink finger sponge.*

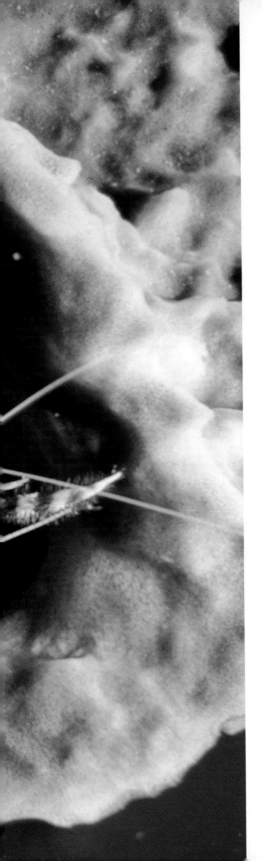

Opposite: *Banded coral shrimps
are found in large barrel sponges
on many dives.*

175

CHARLIES MOUNT

LOCATION: SOUTH COAST
DIVE TYPE: DRIFT REEF
PHOTO TIP: WIDE ANGLE, MID LENS
DEPTH: 60' - 100'
PADO BUOY: YES

Charlies Mount is an extension of the south banking reef and it protrudes out at right angles to the main reef. There is a steep slope on the right or east side while the other side slopes more gently. The top of the reef where the mooring rope is attached lies at 60 feet, close to some large hard coral formations. One of them has a cleaning station serviced by a dozen or so bluehead wrasse. This wrasse is a small fish, the adult having a bright blue head and green body while the juvenile version is completely bright yellow.

Mackerel scad is a fish that schools in numbers and they can be seen rushing about above the reef. They don't feed on the reef and only come down to use cleaning stations, such as the one previously mentioned.

The reef is a garden of hard and soft corals. Look closely among them and it is possible to find large spiny spider crabs, lizardfish, pufferfish, peacock flounders and many other creatures. The common reef fish are present in good supply, but nothing prolific.

There is more brown sponge growth than other kinds, and as such one could say this dive lacks colour.

Opposite: Brown octopus sponge is a common reef feature.
Overleaf: Schooling mackerel scad flash across the reef.

BARBADOS DIVE GUIDE

THE FINGER

LOCATION: SOUTH COAST
DIVE TYPE: DRIFT REEF
PHOTO TIP: CLOSE-UP AND ZOOM
DEPTH: 30' - 80'
PADO BUOY: NO

The site is opposite the Welcome Inn Hotel on the south coast and, as the name suggests, is a finger-shaped reef projecting out from the fringing reef. There is no buoy so a free descent to the top of the reef at 30 feet is necessary, which on most days is observable.

The finger, though only moderately covered in a mixture of hard corals, sea whips, sea plumes and purple sea fans, does give the impression it has been planned by a garden designer. Each kind of sponge adds its own colourful accent and dimension to the reef. With plenty of reef fish such as peacock flounders, damselfish, squirrelfish, yellow and red snapper, grunts and rock beauties, the overall appearance is more than satisfying.

It is usual to begin the dive on the left side, traveling all the way around to the other side. On the left side the reef slopes sharply down to a sandy bottom at 100 feet, and this is the best place to do the deepest part of the dive. There have been sightings of octopus and juvenile hawksbill turtles along here at a depth of 75 feet.

Schools of blue and brown chromis dance above the reef, energetically feeding on passing plankton.

Where the point flattens out and joins the main reef bank the photographic subjects are plentiful. Here in 30 feet there is plenty of time, air permitting, to look for specific marine animals like Highhat fish, pufferfish, scorpionfish, eels and goatfish.

Opposite: *This juvenile hawksbill turtle stares back at me from his coral sanctuary.*
Overleaf: *Scorpion fish laying motionless on the reef.*

GRAEME HALL SHALLOWS

LOCATION: SOUTH COAST
DIVE TYPE: SHALLOW DRIFT REEF
PHOTO TIP: CLOSE-UP AND MID LENS
DEPTH: 50' - 90'
PADO BUOY: NO

This has been described as a bar reef as it is about 400 feet long and 40 feet in width and is not attached to any other reef. Situated a long way down the south coast, near Oistins Bay, this reef is well known by local fishermen.

The top of the reef starts at 50 feet and gradually deepens to 70 feet as you travel west. Both sides slope down to flat sand at a depth of 90 feet. It is advisable not to go too deep for too long at the beginning of the dive or you may end up with a shortened dive.

Once again the reef is covered in soft corals with some large flowing sea plumes and whips that particularly stand out. Trumpet fish thrive along with parrotfish, scrawled filefish, graysby, butterfly fish, trunk fish and other common varieties. turtles and barracuda are attracted to the area, perhaps because of the ample camouflage of barrel sponges and sea fans.

Opposite: *A banded butterfly fish passes by a large barrel sponge.*
Last Page: *The graysby fish is often motionless on the reef, in this pose.*

INDEX

A. Angelfish, 33
  French, 97, **102**, 125
  Queen, 173
 Anemone, **52**, 65, 83, **84**, **167**, 169
 Atlantic Spade Fish, 21, **68**
 Atlantic Squid, 19, 63, 113, 159
 Atlantis Submarine, **26**, 35, 131

B. Bajan Queen Wreck, 135, 137
 Barge, The 35, 137
 Barracuda, 19, 21, **58**, 59, 65, **73**, 101, **124**, 163
  Blackfin, **14**
 Basket Star, 21,27, 143, **145**
 Batfish, 137
 Berwyn, The **23**, 135, 137
 Black Durgon, 95
 Blackbar Soldier Fish, 63, 81, 137
 Blenny, **24**, 75
 Blue Tang, 113, 147
 Boga, 21, 75, 173
 Brittle Star, **44**,
 Butterfly Fish, 35, 95, 112,
  Banded, **184**
  Foureye, **112**
 BSTP, Barbados Sea Turtle Project, 29-31, 30

C. Carlisle Bay, 38
 Carlisle Bay Marine Park Wrecks, 35, 133- 137
 Cero, 67, 169
 Ce-Trek, Wreck 136
 Chamber Recompression, 27
 ChristmasTree Worms, **48**, 57, 71, 113, 117, 135, 139, **153**
 Chromis, 35, 57, 67, 79, 105, **116**, 125, 181
 Chub, 35
 Cleaning Station, 75, 85, 127, 177
 Climate, 9
 Coral,
  Black, 63, **64**, 67, 123, 173
  Brain, 21, 57, 71, 108, 131, 163, **171**
  Branching, 105
  Finger, 91, 151
  Pillar, 21, 105, **106**
  Plate Star, 21, 57
  Star, 24, 71, 131
 Cornwallis, The 137

 Crab,
  Arrow, 52, 105, 109
  Coral, 21, 27, 87, **156**
  Spider, **110**
 Crinoid, 21, 27, **142**
 Crop Over Festival, 13

D. Damselfish, 35, 66, 71, 181
 DAN, Divers Alert Network, 27
 Dive Barbados, 41
 Dive Boat Safari, 49
 Dive Centres, 39
 Dive Sites, 55
 Diving Overview, 15-25
 Dive Shop Ltd, 49-51

E. Eels, 19, 33, 57, 95, 135
  Garden, 65, 165, 169
  Goldentail, **127**
  Green Moray, 57, 59, 101, 125
  Sharptail, **51**
  Spotted, 57, 67, 83, **100**, 143
  Spotted Snake, 105, **107**, 137
 Ellion Wreck, 136

F. Fan, Sea 21, 57, 63, 109, **142**, 163, 185
  Deep Sea Fan, **122**, **155**, 173
  Purple, 66, **81**
 Feather Duster, **77**, **78**, 105, 169
 Fire Worm, 65, 136
 Flamingo Tongue Snail, **20**,
 Flying Gurnard, 65
 Folkstone Marine Park, 33
 Friars Craig, Wreck 23, 147, **149**
 Frogfish, 19, 64, 87, **89**

G. Geology, 9
 Glasseye Snapper, 97, **129**, 139
 Glassy Sweeper, 127, 135, **136**
 Gorgonia, 21, 57, 67, 101, 109, **130**
 Goby, 108
  Peppermint, **115**
 Graysby, 187
 Grunt, 63, 113, 117, 125, **133**, 169

H. Harrison's Cave, 8, 9
 Hazell's Water World, 37
 Hightide, 41-42
 History, 13
 Hogfish, Spanish 57, 59, 105, 117
 Hydroids, 121

J. Jack, 21, 65 ,67, 97, 125, 131
 Jawfish, 33
 Junior PADI, 39

K. Kayaking, 35

L. Lettuce Leaf Slug, **34**, 35, 65
 Lizardfish, 59, 67

Lobster,
    Rock, **25**, 27
    Spiny, 64, 105, **141**
Lord Combermere, Wreck **126**,127

M. Mackerel, 19,65, 67, 173, **179**

N. Night Diving, 25

O. Ocean Adventures, 35
    Octopus, 27, **33**, 95, **134**, 181
    One-on-One, 51-53

P. PADO, 27
    Pamir, The **61**, 63
    Parrotfish, 33, 35, 59, 62, 71, 75,
    97, 105, 113, 117, 185
    Peacock Flounder, 33, **46**, 109,
    151, 181
    Pencil Star 35
    Plumes, Sea **18**, 21, 57, 67, 73,
    93, **96**, 113, 129, 143, 159, 173
    Pufferfish, 86, 181

R. Ray, 57
        Eagle, 19, 21, 87, 105
        Manta, 19
        Sting, 19, **90**, 95, 159, 165
    Recreation, 11
    Reefers & Wreckers, 39-41
    Rock beauty, 57, 59, 135
    Rogers Scuba Shack, 47

S. Safari Boat, 32, 33
    Sand Diver, 79, **108**
    Scrawled Filefish, 67, 71, 95, 97,
    109, 185
    Scorpion Fish, 67, 79, 83, 109,
    183
    Seahorse, 19, 21, 33, **37**, **86**, 101,
    119
    Sea Temperature, 9
    Sennet, **150**
    Sergeant Major Fish, 33, 35, 63,
    125
        Eggs, **62**
    Shrimp, 65
        Banded Coral, 64, 99, 136,
    163, **174**
        Bumblebee, back cover
        Cleaner, 27, 83, **85**, 113
        Mantis, 35
    Snapper, 19, 23, 33, 35, 67, 71,
    75, 137, 181
    Snorkeling, 33,
    Snuba, 36

Spawning, 157
Sponge, 19, 59, 63, 71, 75, 94,
109, 142, 162
    Barrel, 21, 64, 99,105,
    116, 149, 161, 163, 174, **184**
    Branching Antler, 57, **60**
    Brown Octopus, 21, **176**
    Green Finger, 59, 95, 119
    Lavender, 66
    Purple Finger, 57, 99
    Red Encrusting, 41
    Orange Elephant Ear, 57, **58**,
    163, **172**
    Yellow Tube, **16**, 57, **66**, 71,
    104, 125, **168**
Spotted Drum, 95, **138**
Squirrelfish, 33, 35, 59, 113, 117,
139, 147, 181
Starfish, 33, 35
S.S Stavronikita, The Wreck **22**, 23,
121-125
Sugar Cane, 11
Surgeon Fish, 35

T. Tarpon, 19, 97
    Technical Information, 27
    Triplefin Fish, Blackedge, **40**
    Trumpetfish, 15, 35, 63, 97, 113,
    147, **171**
    Trunkfish, **17**, 35, 71
    Tube Worm, 77, 105
    Turtle, 19, 21, 29, 30, 42, 57, 59,
    71, 83, 127, 163
        Green, 29, **158**, 159
        Hawksbill, **28**, 30, **31**, 113,
        146, 149, 159, **180**
        Leatherback, 19, 29

U. Underwater Barbados, 47
    Urchin, Sea 35
        Red Heart, 65
W. West Side Scuba, 43-46
    Whips, Sea 19, 163, 173, 185
    Whitespot Filefish, 59, 95, 97,
    98, **164**
    Wolf, The 137
    Wrasse, Bluehead 75, 177
        Cleaner, 75, 177
        Creole, 18, 21, 35, 67, 79,
        82, 125, 159
    Wrecks, 19, 23, 63, 121, 127, 133

Y. Yellow Goatfish, 19, 57, 64, **75**,
    113, 136, 159

Bold numbers denote a photograph.